THE BOAT NOT TAKEN

THE BOAT NOT TAKEN

*A North Korean Mother
and Her Daughter*

A Memoir

Joanna Choi Kalbus

Betty

SANTA ROSA, CALIFORNIA

This book is a memoir. It reflects the author's present recollections of experience over a period of time. Some names have been changed, some events have been compressed, and some dialogue has been re-created.

Edited by Peg Alford Pursell
Designed by Mike Corrao
Cover photograph courtesy of the author
Author portrait © Katherine Briccetti

Library of Congress Control Number: 2024945605

ISBN 979-8-9877197-9-4 (paperback)
ISBN: 979-8-9898729-0-9 (ebook)

Published by Betty
WTAW Press
PO Box 2825
Santa Rosa, CA 95405
www.wtawpress.org

WTAW Press is a not-for-profit literary press. Betty is an imprint focused on publishing books by women for everyone. This publication is made possible by the generous contributions from individual donors, public arts organizations, and private foundations.

In memory of My Omai, Helen Sung Koo Lee, 1905–1996,
with eternal love and gratitude.

For Lee H. Kalbus: You are always in my heart.

AUTHOR'S NOTE

The Boat Not Taken is my memoir, and as such all the persons I mention are or were known to me. Some names have been changed to protect their privacy.

Romanization of Korean Orthography: Korean romanization changes depending on the front and back words, which is called "word division." What I did about romanization was simply to spell the words phonetically.

CONTENTS

IMMIGRANTS IN AMERICA

AFTER OMAI'S DEATH

RETURN TO ASIA

BACK HOME

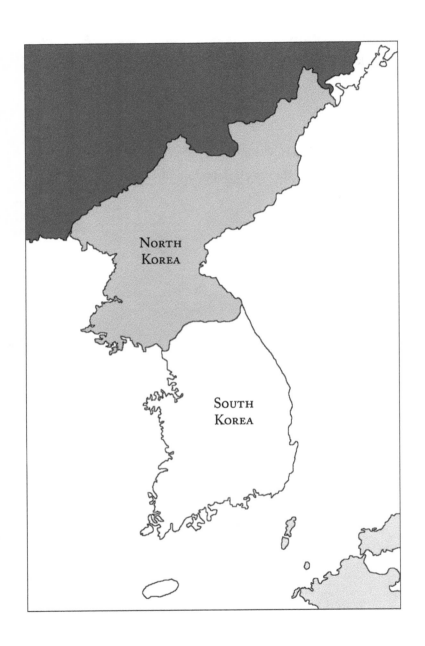

INTRODUCTION

O NE DAY WHEN I was studying a map of Korea, my native country, a song surfaced in my mind, a song my
mother taught me many years ago, "Santoki." One of the
most well-known of Korean children's songs, the lyrics of
"Santoki" in English are: "Mountain rabbit, mountain rabbit, where are you going? Jumping and hopping, where are
you going?" As the song played through my mind, I realized
that Korea, seen as a single whole on the map, looked like the
profile of a mountain rabbit, with its hind legs squatting and
its front paws frozen in a begging position.

An image surfaced of a thick line incising the mountain
rabbit's midsection, severing the body so that the forelegs
could never be in a relaxed, natural position. The line was the
38th parallel, where the global superpowers cut Korea in half
after World War II.

I was born in the part of the rabbit now called North Korea. When I was a child, my mother managed to get us across
the 38th parallel to South Korea. But then the North invaded
the South, and we had to flee again, across a war-ravaged
landscape. I was ten when my mother—my Omai, as I always
called her—got us onto a ship that brought us to the United
States, where I have lived ever since.

Memories are all I have left of my childhood in Korea, and memories are like dreams, like nightmares: they are fragile, fleeting, vague. How much of what I remember comes from experience, how much from stories my mother told me? I do not know. She told her stories in bits and pieces, never bothering to stitch the details together into a single big picture. It never seemed necessary—my life story was safely filed away in my Omai's memories. Anything I needed to know, I could find out from her. She was my life's historian.

Then, on January 17, 1996, my mother, my Omai, my life's historian, died. Only then did I realize how much of my life was a sort of folktale I had constructed from her countless anecdotes. Only then did I realize how little I knew about her life and therefore of my own. I began to understand something was missing from the picture I had formed of our life together. I set out on a quest to discover the truth of my mother's life, and in the course of delving into her story, I discovered my own.

PART 1

THE KOREA YEARS

NEH-CHAI

Unryul, 1915

"WHERE'S NEH-CHAI?" THE VILLAGE children asked. The ten-year-old girl was the established leader of the group. Her nickname meant "number four." She'd been given that nickname because she was the fourth child born to the Lee family in Unryul, Korea.

Neh-chai relished her role as the eldest sister to four younger siblings, and she took good care of them. Her mother lamented that Neh-chai possessed only one feminine trait, devotion to her brothers and sisters.

Lean of build and tall for her age, Neh-chai ventured to do anything that she set her mind to. Even at that young age, she defied gender barriers. One day the children found Neh-chai playing with her two younger brothers in a dirt field. There were eight youngsters under her command. Most of the time, it was Neh-chai who initiated games, activities, and events—events in which she was certain she could excel over others. On this day, a boy challenged her to a contest.

"I bet I can piss longer and higher than you," he boasted.

"You think so?" Neh-chai replied. "We will see about that."

She invited other children to participate. They looked around for a suitable place and found a dirt mound to launch their contest.

Neh-chai, the only girl, lined up with four male participants. Because her anatomy didn't allow her to stand up like the other contestants, she squatted instead, thrusting her pelvis forward and planting her hands on the ground behind her for balance. With bent knees spread wide, her urine streamed into a broad arc before hitting the ground. She out-pissed the boys. Her two little brothers jumped up and down.

"Noona won. Our sister won," they shouted.

When the Lee children went home, the boys rushed to tell their mother the grand feat of their older sister. The women servants clucked their tongues. Her mother sighed and shook her head.

"How are we ever going to marry her off?" she exclaimed.

Neh-chai was my mother, my Omai.

MANSEI

March 1919

NEH-CHAI WAS ONLY FIVE years old when Japan annexed Korea. Before the Japanese invasion, the Lee family had been a prominent clan. Neh-chai's grandfather was the governor of the prefecture. During the occupation, Japan plundered and raped Korea, body and soul. Lands were confiscated; people were forced into harsh labor. Worst of all, the Japanese tried to strip Koreans of their culture, language, and ancestral names.

When Neh-chai was fourteen, Korean nationalists declared their country's independence. That declaration set off widespread demonstrations against Japanese rule. One chilly March day, Grandfather Lee woke up early, dressed in his white baggy pants and full-sleeved shirt, and ate a breakfast served by his wife. Neh-chai had heard that there would be a demonstration in the village center that day. She peeked into Grandfather's room, waiting for an opportunity to ask if she could accompany him to town.

"Will you be gone all day?" her grandmother asked him.

"It appears so." He took a last sip of his barley tea.

Grandfather rose from the floor. Grandmother brought him his topcoat and black stovepipe hat and helped him put on the coat. He went to the front stoop where his shoes were placed, facing outward, and slipped his feet into them.

"Return safely," Grandmother said.

As Grandfather crossed the courtyard, Neh-chai sprang forth.

"Harabuji (Grandfather), may I go with you to town?" she asked.

"No, child. Today's events are not for children." He opened the gate and went out.

Neh-chai waited until she could see only a speck of her grandfather. Then she followed him. When he neared the town center, she quickened her steps. If he had turned around, he would have seen his granddaughter trailing behind him like a shadow.

The crowd thickened in the town center. It was time Neh-chai let her grandfather know she was following him. She ran to catch up.

"Harabuji, don't get mad. I want to see what's happening today. Please let me stay with you."

He wasn't pleased but he knew her well, his independent-minded granddaughter.

"You stay close to me, you understand?" he said in a stern tone.

"Truly, I will," she promised.

Grandfather Lee and Neh-chai entered an inn where he met with other elders of the community in a private room. Neh-chai sat at a table in the main room of the inn. Near her, a dozen or so young men and women were engaged in a lively discussion. She watched their earnest faces and agitated gestures and listened to their loud voices. A young woman, her hair parted straight in the middle and one thick braid descending to her waist, grabbed a thick handful of chopsticks. She plunked them down, on end, in the middle of the table.

They stood erect. Everyone stopped talking.

"Look at these chopsticks. By themselves, they cannot stand alone. But in a bunch together, they stand up. Like these chopsticks, individually, we will fail. Collectively, we will prevail."

She let her words sink in. Together, the others rose and linked their arms in solidarity.

That young woman became Neh-chai's heroine.

Grandfather Lee finished his meeting and they left the inn. Outside, the masses were marching, young and old, waving the forbidden Korean flag. Neh-chai wondered how they had obtained the flags, as Japan had outlawed nationalist items. The marchers chanted in unison Mansei! over and over: Long Live Korea!

Neh-chai wanted to join the march, but Grandfather pushed her back. The police descended upon the demonstrators, and Grandfather turned to her, put his hands on her shoulders, and said, "Run home, Neh-chai. Now! I will be back before dusk."

This time, she obeyed her grandfather.

That evening, however, Grandfather's dinner turned cold.

THE NEXT DAY, WORD came that Grandfather, along with other leaders, was in jail. Many stories were told of that day, and one of them became a legend. Among the hordes of demonstrators, most of whom were men, a young woman stood out. When she spoke, she evoked passion and stirred patriotism in the crowd, even among the older men. The Japanese police chose to make her an example of what others could expect should they continue their demonstrations.

Armed with clubs, the policemen beat the demonstrators out of their way until they reached the girl. Amidst shouts and melee, they dragged her out of the crowd. Other protestors tried to hold onto her, but eventually they had to let go. All the while, the girl shouted, "Mansei!"

At the police station, the Japanese officers stripped her clothes off, shoved a rubber hose between her legs, and turned on the water full force. Her insides burst. She died screaming.

Neh-chai wondered if this martyr was the girl she had seen the day before, the one with the long braid and the bunch of chopsticks. Her heroine forever.

COMING OF AGE

Unryul, 1921

NEH-CHAI'S LIFE REVOLVED AROUND cycles—lunar cycles, seasonal cycles, and more. She was nearing puberty now. In the olden days, maidens were under the guidance of married women who, over the generations, prepared the girls for womanhood and instructed them in female topics such as menstruation.

The year she was fifteen, her mother and girlfriends warned her of a coming monthly event—the menstrual cycle. She waited. As if she were hatching an egg, she put on a rag to hasten the process. Nothing happened. Was something wrong with her body? Her mother worried also, as she herself had borne a child when she was fifteen.

It was common for families to marry off their sons when they were mere boys since the purpose of a marriage was to enhance the family's status through arranging the best terms, such as a large dowry and a bride from a reputable lineage. Neh-chai's mother had married her husband when he was nine years old.

Seasons guided life in the village. For women, summer and fall were the busiest times, devoted to preparing for winter. Like all teenaged girls, Neh-chai helped the women with the work that needed to be done before the season's end.

One of her favorite chores was the trek to nearby mountains to dig up dandelion plants, which had many uses. She loved the taste of the tender leaves, sautéed and seasoned with sesame oil and soy sauce.

On Dandelion Day, the house stirred with excitement and anticipation. The servants prepared kimbap—rice wrapped in seaweed—for a picnic lunch. Grandmother supervised preparations for the outing, while her daughter-in-law, Neh-chai's mother, carried out the old woman's commands.

Before the sun topped the mountain, the women and children of the household piled into an ox-driven cart. They sang songs as the lumbering beast trudged along, swishing its tail in rhythmic motion. When they reached their destination, everyone spilled out, carrying baskets of stiff bamboo reeds or straw.

This Dandelion Day, Neh-chai followed a path deep into the forest, her younger sister trailing behind. Through patches in the trees, bright sunlight sprinkled the leaves with a palette of verdant hues. As they scrambled up the steep mountainside, soft breezes brushed their faces, which were flushed from the exertion of climbing.

"How far up are we going, On-nee (Big Sister)?" Neh-chai's little sister asked.

"Just a bit more," she said.

"I am tired. I see dandelion plants right here. Couldn't we dig up these ones?" the child whined.

"Look at them, Soong Bong. They're so small and the leaves are lusterless. Don't you want to find the big ones?" Neh-chai took her sister by the hand and walked on.

Finally, she found the right place.

"This is it!" She crouched and thrust her shovel into the soil to uproot a large dandelion plant.

Soong Bong watched and grimaced. "How can you dig that up? It's next to a big pile of dung!"

"Little Sister, it is because of the dung that this plant is so healthy. Look at the dark green color of the leaves. Sometimes, if you want the best, you have to withstand some unpleasantness."

Gingerly, Soong Bong dug up a plant, grimacing. She spat and blurted, "I am going to be sick!"

Neh-chai simply kept filling her basket—and Soong Bong's—with dandelion plants. Then they lugged them back down the mountainside. Neh-chai repeated her grandfather's words:

From ugliness arises beauty. Out of sadness comes happiness. Out of darkness comes light.

WINTER CAME BUT NEH-CHAI's large family was well prepared. Many barrel-sized earthen jars containing kimchi had been placed underground before the ground froze; dried vegetables and fruits as well as grains were shelved in the pantry.

Winters were severe in Unryul. Everyone looked forward to spring, the season when nature springs to life again. Neh-chai looked forward to picking young bracken ferns (kosari). Families would scour the mountains for them. Each spring, Neh-chai filled her large basket with the fiddleheads to make stir-fried kosari for a special occasion.

And the special occasion came that spring. At the age of sixteen, Neh-chai became a woman—at last.

THE FAMILY PORTRAIT

Unryul, 1923

"Goh-keoh, goh-keoh."
The rooster blared his wake-up call, announcing the dawning of another day. Neh-chai sat up on her bedroll. Her two younger sisters sleeping next to her on the floor stirred. She stood and hopped over them. As the oldest sister, she had many responsibilities. Her first task this morning was to get her two brothers ready for today's important event.

She opened the sliding paper door to their room and entered. The smaller of the two boys sprawled like a dead frog on top of his bedroll, snoring. Hidden under a mound of blankets, the older one could not be seen. How typical of them both!

"Wake up," she shouted. "Don't you know what today is? It's picture-taking day. The photographer is coming all the way from Pyongyang."

The older brother slithered out from under his covers like a seal.

"What?" the sleep-dazed younger one spluttered. "What are you saying?"

"Wake up! It's picture day!" Neh-chai pulled their blankets off. She folded them and again ordered her brothers to get up.

THE FAMILY LINED UP in the inner courtyard of the main house. In the front row—befitting their positions in the family—sat Grandfather and Grandmother. On either side of them, the boys took their places. In the back row, Mother and Father stood behind the grandparents. The two older daughters stood next to their father, and the youngest one hung onto her mother.

Everybody wore their New Year's Day outfits, their best clothes. The two younger girls had on identical blouses with multicolored sleeves and long skirts. Neh-chai wore a long blue skirt and a pink silk blouse, trimmed with blue borders around the neckline and sleeves. Her hair, parted in the middle, was plaited into a thick braid threaded with a bright red ribbon.

She stood tall and looked straight at the camera perched on a tripod in front of her. A body stood behind it. A black hood covered the photographer's head, and his arms, like appendages to the instrument, fiddled with what appeared to be a light bulb attached to a small pump.

The family waited in silence. Finally, the photographer lifted the cloth from his head and emerged from behind. He was young and dressed in a Western suit. Everything about him gave him the aura of a citified person. One glance at him took Neh-chai's breath away. He approached her assembled family and addressed Neh-chai in the third person.

"Will Honorable Daughter please move to the center?" he requested and orchestrated the placement. Neh-chai did as she was told and stood still as a statue, avoiding eye contact with him.

After he adjusted the positions of other family members, he returned to his equipment. His head disappeared under the black cloth.

"Look over here," he said, his voice muffled. He waved his left hand. "On the count of three, I am going to take the picture."

Little did Neh-chai know that the picture-taking was an interview with destiny. The photographer was deciding whether or not to marry her.

He did!

ESCAPE TO CHINA

Pyongyang, 1930

NEH-CHAI LEFT HER VILLAGE at nineteen to become the wife of Chang-sik, the youngest son of the Choi family in Pyongyang. Though he had posed as a photographer in order to get a good look at her before their marriage, he was a physician. A year after the wedding, Neh-chai fulfilled her duty to them by delivering a son. Now, befitting her raised status, she was referred to as Aggie Omoni, Baby's Mother. One evening, an evening that started like any other, she waited for her husband to come home. Nearby, her child slept on his bed quilt.

In the middle of the common room, a low table was set with Chang-sik's dinner. Neh-chai touched the two silver bowls on the lacquer tray to see if they were still warm. One contained rice, the other seaweed soup. She placed a square linen cloth over the food. Her husband should have been home from work two hours ago.

Then she heard his familiar footsteps. They seemed heavier this evening.

"Please," she said, as she slid the paper and bamboo sliding door open. "Come in."

"I am sorry I am late," her husband said. His brows were furrowed.

"Is anything wrong?"

Chang-sik sat on the floor facing his dinner. He took off his glasses and closed his eyes for a moment. Neh-chai waited.

"Kyung-sik shot a Japanese policeman," he whispered.

"Aigoo! Your brother shot a policeman?" she exclaimed. "What happened?"

"He had no choice. It is done," Chang-sik said. "Now we have to deal with the situation." He rubbed his temples, as if that would eradicate his eldest brother's action.

They did not need to say more. Both knew the severity of such a crime. Under Japanese rule, killing a Japanese policeman meant that the entire Choi family was in jeopardy. For two decades Koreans had been without a country, thus without citizenship, and they were subject to whatever punishment the Emperor of the Japanese Empire might wish to mete out.

That night, Neh-chai wrote a letter to her parents. Kneeling by the writing table, she composed her thoughts as she dipped her pen into the inkwell.

To FATHER AND MOTHER whom I wish to see very much,

I hope this letter finds all the family to be in good health. We are well. Your grandson is a gentle boy. I am writing to let you know a recent incident involving a family member makes it impossible for us to live here.

Please do not worry, Father and Mother. I will write again when we get settled.

Respectfully,

Your Daughter

NEH-CHAI PUT HER PEN down and blew on the paper to dry the ink. She replaced the cap on the pen and the lid on the inkwell.

The next forty-eight hours felt as if she lived in two worlds: one filled with the silent frenzy of her mind, the other with the day's ordinary routines. On this last night in their home, while she waited for her husband to come home, she surveyed in her mind the preparations for their departure: two overcoats padded with cotton for her husband and herself and two sets of cotton-filled outfits for her son that she had made for their escape. In the overcoats, she had sewn secret pockets to store their valuables.

Neh-chai had selected only the most essential items for the journey, and packed just two small suitcases with items culled from an entire household of goods. With those two bags, they would start a new life in an unknown foreign country: Manchuria.

Her husband arrived home long past dusk. She watched him mechanically shove a morsel of rice into his mouth with his chopsticks. He had aged in just two days. Chang-sik pushed up his round rimless spectacles every few seconds, a newly acquired nervous habit. His brother's action had upended the world for the entire family. The imminent possibility of being executed or sent to forced labor camps loomed.

Chang-sik picked at his dinner, and after drinking his barley tea, he stood and noticed a letter on the writing table. He picked it up to read while Neh-chai began to clear the dinner table.

"Yuh-bo, what do you think you are doing, writing this letter?" He flailed the piece of rice paper in front of her face. His tone was as thin as the paper and the sliver of his sharp voice cut into her. "Do you have any idea what would happen if this letter got into the wrong hands?" It was not a question.

Neh-chai stood quietly, but her heartbeat matched her booming pulse. Chang-sik crumpled the flimsy paper in one hand and threw it in her direction.

"Burn it," he ordered, as he stormed out to the inner courtyard.

Neh-chai stooped to pick up the paper ball. She smoothed it flat and folded it until it fit into her palm. She slid it in a hidden pocket of her underclothes. That night, they left—a family that would be uprooted more than once by violence and sent scrambling for safety.

REMEMBRANCES OF
NORTH KOREA

Unryul, 1944

A T WHAT AGE DO we first begin to remember things? My earliest memories go back to when I was three. For a transplanted Korean, a person's exact age is hard to determine. In the Korean custom, everyone turns a year older on the Lunar New Year's Day. I was born in August, so after four months of life, I became one year old.

Are these memories mixed with imagination and marinated in stories told over the years? My earliest recollections of my life in North Korea resemble a well-worn album of faded photos composed in a sporadic style. Images such as me sitting atop a tall watchtower in a watermelon patch, eating watermelon, me at the river with the women and other children, a big house with a slate-tiled roof, guarded by high walls and many gates.

I saw a replica of my first home at the Lotte Department Store in Seoul, South Korea, when I visited decades later. The store had a permanent exhibition of ancient villages. When I identified my village, forgotten memories flooded my mind.

All the villagers knew the house where my family lived. It belonged to Grandfather and Big Uncle, Grandfather's eldest son. The entire extended family lived under the same roof. My immediate family consisted of my mother, my two older brothers, and me.

I referred to the elder of my two brothers as Big Brother and the other as Little Brother. I didn't see much of Big Brother since he attended a boarding school. Whenever he came home for the holidays, my mother labored all day preparing his favorite foods. Every day was a feast day for as long as he was home.

The dining table overflowed with a variety of panchan (side dishes). During dinner, Little Brother hunted for hidden delicacies of buried eggs in the dumpling soup. When he found an egg, my mother, ever watchful, took that dish away and placed it closer to her number one son. This didn't deter Little Brother. He would just reach farther and eat faster than Big Brother. That might explain why Little Brother was bigger.

Since Korean custom dictates that men and boys eat at the table while women serve them, girls and young boys are left to their own devices. I had no difficulty keeping myself entertained. One hot summer evening, I found a half of a watermelon with the inside hollowed out. A perfect helmet. I scooped out the rest of the watermelon flesh and lined the inside with crumpled newspaper. Then I crowned my head with my new creation.

Wanting to show off my helmet, I began to cross over the low dining table. Big Brother looked up with chopsticks poised in midair. He looked at me with astonishment bordering on sternness.

He called our mother, pointing to what I am sure he thought of as a spectacle, a three-year-old girl wearing nothing but a watermelon helmet.

"Doesn't she know any better than to put a watermelon on her head?"

I had a feeling he wanted our mother to banish me as if I were leftover food that needed to be cleared from the table. I removed my huge fruit hat and shoved it close to his face. "See, there's no juice," I said. "I stuffed newspaper inside." I peeled away the paper to reveal the white rind. "No mushy watermelon in my hat."

Big Brother's mouth turned crooked on one side. I took that as a smile. I imagine I was happy to get his approval, as he was practically an adult at age nineteen to my three years of age.

I was close to Little Brother who was eight years older than I. Often he babysat me. I don't recall where my mother was when Little Brother was in charge of me. He carried me on his back, and we both liked this arrangement. He, a boy of eleven, was constantly in a hurry, and I enjoyed being able to talk with him and, best of all, join in on all of his activities.

Often, he'd take me to town. One day I was so cranky that I didn't even like the piggyback ride. I wanted to go home to my mother. To distract me, Little Brother told me stories. We approached a brick building with windows fitted with iron bars. We peered through one of the windows, between the bars.

He turned his head sideways toward me, and in a low voice whispered, "Look in there. What do you see?"

I focused my attention on the darkness behind the iron grille.

"I can't see anything," I whispered.

He told me there was a dungeon deep down inside the building where a ferocious dragon lived. When the dragon breathed, fire came out of his nostrils. He said, "If you are really quiet, you can hear it breathing."

I tightened my grip on his neck. Goose bumps had risen on my arms.

"The mean dragon is asleep. If you make any noise, you will wake it up," my brother said. His voice had grown even more hushed. He walked closer to where the dragon was sleeping.

I opened my eyes wide so that I, too, could see the sleeping monster in the black pit. Then I snapped them closed, afraid that if I looked, the dragon would wake up. Heart pounding, I asked my brother, "Is he still asleep?"

"The dragon is about to wake up," he said. "You have to be very quiet. We have to sneak out of here before it wakes."

Dusk had given way to evening by the time we left the abandoned building behind. All the way home, I kept turning around to see if the dragon was chasing us.

THE PART OF OUR home I remember most vividly is the large courtyard that served as a community of its own. All summer and fall, women prepared for winter by drying fruits and vegetables in the open area. My grandmother made the rounds, inspecting the vegetables drying on straw mats strewn on the courtyard ground. I followed her, imitating the way she walked, bending my body forward with my arms behind my back. Each day the uniformly cut white radishes shriveled to curlicues on the straw mats.

Making kimchi took many weeks and the work of many hands. Grandmother and I supervised the women of the household as they took their posts in the courtyard. I counted the varieties of kimchi. Po-kimchi was made of whole cabbage stuffed with white radishes sliced into slivers. This differed from chopped cabbage kimchi and from moo kimchi made of white radishes and cucumbers.

"This is chongkak kimchi," my grandmother said.

"Halmoni, why is it called chongkak?" I asked.

Grandmother laughed. Her mouth looked like a baby's as she had only one bottom tooth. She was a short woman but appeared even shorter because she walked with a perpetual stoop as if she were carrying an invisible child on her back, accentuated by her bowlegs.

"It's called chongkak because the radishes are very small, as you can see."

That evening, I asked my mother the same question.

"Chongkak," she said, "means . . . a yet-to-be-married young lad."

I wondered what that had to do with kimchi. It took years before I appreciated my grandmother's sense of humor, a tiny white radish belonging to a boy.

Like assembly line workers, the women soaked, chopped, and mixed the ingredients and packed them into great pot-bellied earthen jars. In the meantime, the men dug deep holes in the ground to store the jars. The cold of the frozen ground preserved the kimchi during the barren season.

Living with maternal grandparents, an uncle and his family, and housekeepers and other assorted servants, I never questioned being fatherless. No one ever talked about it until one day at the river.

In the summer, we children enjoyed going to the riverbank with the womenfolk, where we'd get to bathe and frolic in the cool, refreshing water. Ajumma—"aunts," as the children addressed all women in Korea—walked erect, a blanket mound full of laundry balanced on their heads. The older children ran ahead while we little ones held on to our mothers' hands.

At the river, the women scouted around for a favorite rock. My mother chose a large, flat one. She jimmied it into position, slanting it so the lower end dipped into the continuous river flow. These human laundry machines squatted for hours washing clothes. My mother soaked each piece of clothing and then lathered it with homemade lye soap. She used a wooden paddle to beat the garments—a primitive version of an agitator in a washing machine. The pounding of the women's paddles blended into syncopated rhythm.

During the rinse cycle, the launderers stood ankle-deep in water, flapping their laundry in the running water over and over until it ran clear. Next, they wrung the laundry into tight ropes. There wasn't a drop of water in our clothing by the time my mother got through with them. She then located bushes that received full sun. There, she laid out her sparkling laundry across the branches, the whites blinding in the sunlight.

Doing hand laundry took all day and respite came only during the drying cycle. The tired workers gathered together and talked, gossiping about their neighbors. It was then when, on that fateful day, I heard a woman discussing my mother's widowhood. She told her listeners that it must be hard living without a husband and with three children to raise.

Others in the group clucked their tongues in agreement, unaware that I was eavesdropping. Even at the age of three, I intuited the discussion was not complimentary to my mother. Why did they speak in hushed tones? Why were they clucking their tongues? Why were they talking about my mother when she wasn't present?

"I feel sorry for the little girl," one woman said, "growing up without a father."

I stepped out in front of them. "Don't feel sorry for me!" I blurted. "Why would I need a father when I have my mother?"

The gossipers were taken aback.

"Aiyee," an older one said. "Just listen to her! Imagine such words coming out of such a young thing."

No one responded. There was only silence. I turned and went to find my mother.

The following day, the women described their version of the incident to her.

Overnight, my reputation had become enhanced. The legend grew, and I was known thereafter as aureun-ai. Adult-child.

IN THE EVENINGS, I belonged to my mother. She and I slept in the same bedding on the floor. I suckled her swollen breast, careful to keep my teeth from grating her nipple. During the day, I was "the adult-child" but at night, I was not just a child, I was a baby.

In the darkness of the communal room, our ritual continued. Close to my fourth birthday, I discussed our nightly habit with my mother. "Omai, I don't want to have milk anymore. It doesn't taste good."

"How true! You eat kimchi and compared to it, the milk must be bland," she said.

So I stopped nursing, but we continued to sleep together, my Omai and I, right up to my wedding day.

I understand my mother's feelings now. She wanted to prolong and savor her motherhood. I was her mak-neh: her last one.

KŪT FOR
GRANDFATHER

ONE EVENING, WHEN I was around four, the sound of a drumbeat from inside our house came to me in the courtyard. The papered wooden sliding door was open to the common room in the main house. I followed the sound into the common room, where the four walls were decorated with cloth banners imprinted with calligraphy. A long, low table next to the center wall was covered with a resplendent array of offerings: pyramids of fruits, including shiny red apples next to bright yellow oranges in alternate rows. In front, rice cakes of different sizes, shapes, and colors were piled high on lacquered plates.

Yellow lights from the hanging lanterns flickered to the beat of the drum. No one saw me enter since so many people were sitting on the floor with their backs to the walls. They gave their attention to a woman who danced and sang in the middle of the room. She wore a traditional Korean costume, but one much more elaborate than I had ever seen, long flowing garments of many layers and multiple colors: a yellow blouse, a long blue skirt, and a red topcoat with six panels that swirled like a pinwheel as she whirled. A square-shaped black headdress with tassels sat on the crown of her head.

When she spun around and around to the beat of the jangoo, a Korean drum, she looked like a rainbow-colored spinning top. The musicians accompanying her sat in a corner. Besides the drummer, there were a reed player and a cymbalist. Surrounding the musicians were folks with bells, constantly jingling them to the drumbeat. The woman's movements mirrored their rhythmic beats. Hearing the pounding beat of the drum accompanied by the striking of the cymbals made my heart pound harder than when I listened to the ghost stories Little Brother told. I found my mother and sat next to her.

The drummer sat cross-legged, the jangoo, with its two drums on each side, in front of him. He doubled the tempo, drumming the left drum with his hand, while tapping the right drum with a bamboo stick, faster and faster. The dancer made jerky movements with her shoulders and arms, all the while keeping up with the rhythm by bobbing up and down to her knees.

"Omai, what's happening?" I asked, cupping my hands to my mouth as I whispered close to my mother's ear.

"Kūt hahn dah. (We are having a kūt.) Kūt is a ceremony where the mudang (dancer-singer) talks to the gushin (spirits)."

My mother didn't take her eyes off of the mudang. The drumbeat got faster and faster, the clanging of the cymbals louder and louder, the reed pipe's notes shriller and shriller. The dancer was no longer a woman but a life-size spinning top.

I shivered when she spoke of gushin. Omai often told me stories about these invisible spirits. If I did something bad, they would come and take me away. I did not want to be anywhere near such spirits.

Suddenly, the mudang started wailing.

"Is she hurt?" I asked.

Without looking at me, my mother replied, "No. She is singing to the spirits."

Her singing was more akin to the shrill howling of a cat. I couldn't calm my beating heart. Just as I had entered the Kūt ceremony without notice, I left my mother's side and ran to our house on the other side of the family compound. Trails of the incessant cacophony—drumbeats, clanging of the cymbals, the wails of the mudang—followed me. Only after I closed the sliding door was I able to take a deep breath of relief.

The clamorous ceremony lasted three days. It finally came to an end when the mudang went into a trance and passed out.

When I was older, I learned that mudangs are shamans who are able to channel spirits. What I witnessed that day was a séance where the mudang implored the spirit powers to heal my ailing grandfather, who later recovered.

In the years that followed, I'd often hear my mother utter, "Kūt geut nango kah teh (It seems kūt has ended)" whenever something hectic or chaotic was over. But I doubt she ever believed that kūt had really ended for good.

ESCAPE FROM
NORTH KOREA

Yalu Sea, 1946

A s a child I wondered how the moon knew where I was going. It followed me everywhere. The first time the moon became my companion and guide was in 1946. The Communists had taken over after what should have been a happy and historical event in the history of Korea: liberation from almost half a century of occupation by the Japanese. That, however, was the year world leaders divided Korea into two parts. North Korea became a communist country and South Korea a newborn democracy.

I often heard adults talk about Hitulah, Mussolini, Sutalin, Roosuberutu. Only Mussolini's name was pronounceable by the Koreans, as Korean is a syllabic language in which a consonant is always followed by a vowel. Many years later I deciphered the other famous foreign names of Hitler, Stalin, and Roosevelt.

My family fled the North after the Communist regime parceled out all our vast landholdings to the sharecroppers. In the stealth of night, my mother, my second brother, and I joined six others at a pier. Unbeknownst to me, as I was only five years old, these people, my mother included, must have made extensive preparations for our flight. We boarded a small rickety boat. I recall my mother and brother struggling to load aboard, of all things, a grandfather clock.

The moon was full and its reflection on the sea washed the dark waters with a syrupy glaze of golden sheen. Moving about swiftly, everyone spoke in hushed tones. Just like birds I'd seen in flight, communicating silently, the little group worked in concert and then settled in their places in the boat. I sat next to my mother. The only sounds were the ebb-and-flow slushing of the waves.

Suddenly the half-hour chime of our grandfather clock startled us all. My mother quickly grabbed my brother's hand and reached over to the clock.

"Hold onto the boo-ral," she whispered, pointing to the pendulum. Throughout the trip, my brother held onto the clock's boo-ral (testicle).

My mother finally relaxed her hold on me. We let the silence lull us, each of us lost in private thoughts. Abruptly, a shushed, yet clipped, voice said, "We have a leak." Everyone turned toward the voice. He pointed to where the water had started to pool. In the midst of our escape, the boat had sprung a leak!

"Do we have something to cork the hole?" another man said in a low voice.

The oarsmen continued to row. One turned and said, "Use your clothes. Do it quickly!"

The men took off their shirts and stuffed them into the hole. The quiet frenzy to plug the leak turned the other passengers into statues frozen in fear. Afraid of sinking to death, afraid of being discovered by the police, and afraid of not escaping. Afraid.

After that, every sound, every rustle muffled our breath. The sound of oar-churned water was like an alarm to guide the border patrol to our boat.

Everyone monitored the stuffed hole. Water started to seep up through the clothing. The oarsmen rowed faster. Men took turns rowing. The rest of us sat stonily, the moonlight reflecting off our faces while our feet were cemented in the cold and rising water. My mother, my brother, and I huddled together for warmth and comfort. I put my head on my mother's bosom and looked up at the moon far above us in the dark sky.

OUR BATTERED BOAT DOCKED at dawn in the port town of Inchon, South Korea. We arrived on the shores before the sunrise, uncertain what the new day would bring.

My mother carried me on her back. Everything was so different from our village. The ocean breeze blew a pungent smell of fish near the docks. Large platforms were loaded with wooden crates. I had never seen so many people. Gruff-looking men shouting orders; soldiers with guns slung over their shoulders. Their uniforms looked different than the ones I had seen.

"Look, Omai. The Russians look different here," I whispered to my mother.

"Over here, they are not Russians. These soldiers are Yankees," she said.

At that age, I didn't know the difference.

Then came my first taxi ride. My mother told me to get into a car that had stopped to pick up more passengers even though the car was already full. Two rows of seats faced each other. Taller persons' knees touched others' knees. No one seemed to mind, and the driver jammed in many more passengers until we appeared glued together. I rode squeezed between my mother and a large man. I stretched my neck to see the city landscape pass by: so many buildings, cars honking, bicyclists blasting their horns, men stooped under the weight of portable A-frame thatched carts on their backs. The bumpy ride lulled me to sleep. I woke at the sound of a faint voice.

"Woon-hee yah, wake up. We are here. We are in Seoul." It was my mother's voice, but that familiar voice, my Omai's voice, sounded tentative, as if a question mark followed her words. Her speech was so slow and weary that even half asleep, I wondered now what? Looking at my mother's haggard face, I did not ask that question out loud. But the answer came soon enough: now, the struggle to survive.

THE BOAT NOT TAKEN

Seoul, 1946

M Y MOTHER, A WOMAN of gentility, had no means of supporting herself, my thirteen-year-old brother, and me. It was also a time, and still is in certain parts of the world, when males were more valued than females. So, my brother was taken in by a distant relative. Now, there were only the two of us, but we had next to no money. When our money ran out, we sold the treasured grandfather clock that had kept us company on the boat. I cannot recall the many places where we slept. Even so, as long as I had my mother, nothing mattered.

We stayed with other refugees from our province. Everything in the boardinghouse was communal, including the old-fashioned iron. One day, my mother took apart her long blue silk skirt and used it to make a pleated skirt for me. I watched her make each pleat the same width. She heated the small, heavy iron on the grill of the kitchen hearth. She tested the heat of the iron by spitting on the plate. When it sizzled, she ironed the pleats into knife-sharp creases. When I tried the skirt on, I looked as though I were wrapped in a perfect fan.

The next day, my mother told me to wear the skirt and a sailor blouse. We must be going to someplace special, I thought. I looked in my little drawstring purse for the ruby ring Grandmother had given me before we left our hometown. I couldn't find it.

When my mother returned to braid my hair, I asked if she'd seen my ring. She put the comb down. Threading the blue ribbon between her fingers, she gazed at me for a long moment.

"Someday, I will get you another ruby ring," she said.

THAT MORNING WHEN WE stepped outside, the sun was so bright, I shielded my eyes with my right hand. A perfect day for an outing. I held Omai's hand and skipped to keep up with her fast pace. Along the way, I pinched my nose when a weather-beaten "dung man" passed by, balancing on his bony shoulders a long bamboo stick with a bucket full of human waste at each end of the pole. He teetered, so heavy was his load. Although I couldn't smell the contents, I heard the slush-slush slurping sound with his every step.

It didn't take long for me to trip on the street's uneven pavement. I caught myself just in time to save my new skirt from dirt.

"Shall I carry you on my back?" my mother offered, arranging the pleats of my skirt. I nodded.

From the comfort of riding on her back, I asked, "Where are we going, Omai?" She stopped and turned her head to the left to catch my gaze, and I stretched my neck and tilted my head to face her.

"We are going to visit the soonyeo (nuns). You remember them from our church in Unryul, don't you? You are going to stay with them for a little while." I saw only my mother's profile. She used her low voice, not her high, trilling voice. I heard the word chokkum (little). I would be staying with the nuns "a little while." On her back, so close to her, I could hear her breathing. Staying at the convent for a little while didn't seem too bad. Besides, I didn't have to worry about it at that moment since it would be much later in the day, way in the future.

We arrived at a large building in another section of the city. I didn't know how to read the sign above the entrance. My mother rang the bell. I held her hand as we stood at the door. A woman wearing a black flowing garment, with a string of beads wrapped around her waist for a belt, opened the door. Her face looked like the center of a sunflower, surrounded as it was by a white pleated circular fan. I wondered if she had hair under the head covering.

"How are you, Mother Superior?" my mother said and bowed.

"Do come in. This must be your daughter," the woman said.

The two talked for a few moments. I looked around and saw more "mother superiors." Later, I found out that the other black-clad women were addressed as "Sister," some as "Mother," but there was only one "Mother Superior."

Sister Maria was to be my surrogate mother. She took my mother and me to a large room that housed the girls. I was to be one of them. This was where I'd be staying. I swallowed a gob of saliva. My mother handed a kerchief bundle to Sister Maria. I hadn't even noticed the small pouch until that moment. The nun placed it inside an empty cubbyhole. That must be my clothes, I thought. I didn't ask, but I made sure I memorized where the bundle was. I didn't like the situation, and yet, since it was my mother who brought me here, it must be all right. Nevertheless, I held onto her hand firmly.

The time came for my mother to say goodbye. She crouched down to face me.

"I will come back for you as soon as I can. You know that, don't you?"

"I know." I wanted to shout that I didn't want to stay here. I wanted to grab her and cry, "Please don't leave me!" Instead, I lowered my head and looked down at the pleats of my skirt.

"You are a very smart girl. Mind the Sisters," my mother said, folding my hands in hers.

"Come back soon, Omai. I will be waiting." These words came out of my mouth—like a parrot's words. My cold hands were enclosed within Omai's warm hands.

Before the tears flowed, Sister Maria whisked me away to help her with her chores. I wanted my mother to be proud of me. During the day, whenever possible, I tagged along after Sister Maria. For the first days at the orphanage, she would feed me. She knew I liked dumpling soup. She'd take each dumpling and break it into bite-size pieces. I thought of Omai's mandoo (dumpling) she made especially for me. She rolled the dough flat and used a small soju cup to cut out the circular "skin." Each mandoo was a perfect size to fit in my mouth.

The other dish I liked was kimbap. Omai brushed sesame oil onto each sheet of seaweed and sprinkled salt over it. Then, she seared each thin seaweed laver lightly over a low flame. She cut it into tiny squares with scissors and methodically filled each one with a spoonful of hot rice. She squeezed the edges together to make walnut-sized kimbap, just for me. Sister Maria didn't have the time to do that. She'd slap a huge glob of rice on an any-sized seaweed sheet and plop it on my plate. I had to roll my own kimbap. Still, the meals with Sister Maria were the only time I didn't feel lonely.

In the evening, I'd wait until each girl was settled on her cot and the nun in charge closed the door to our room. In the darkness, I heard a girl singing and the big girl next to me breathing through her mouth. I held my soft bundle to my chest and lay on my left side, the same position I had slept in with my mother. I hadn't suckled her breast for a year now but we still slept with her right arm underneath my head, which faced her right breast, and my right hand pressed on her other breast. I clutched the bag tighter. Tears streamed down my face, but I kept my mouth shut so that the shuddering sounds from deep inside of me could not escape. I wondered where my mother was at that moment. Was my Omai far away like the sound of the train whistle I heard each night? In the quiet of the night, the train too seemed to be crying.

Every day I waited for my mother. I had my little bundle of clothes packed and ready to go. I kept time by the routine of the day. Time to eat, time to clean up, time to play. Whenever I could, I'd stare out the window wishing Omai would appear. Every time the doorbell rang, I'd stop what I was doing and peek to see who was at the door, even after another girl told on me for not doing my share of washing the floor. At the convent, even little children like me had to scrub the floor of our communal room. We'd all line up at one end of the room, each child with a wet rag. Then, on cue, we'd move on all fours, our hands scrubbing the floor with the rag as our feet walked our bodies forward.

How long did I stay at the orphanage? I don't know, but long enough to get my bangs cut twice when they covered my eyes, long enough that I no longer had the blue ribbon to weave into my two braids, as no one had any time to groom me. Long enough to find out that the nuns do have hair. But not long enough to call Sister Maria Omoni (Mother), like all the other little girls did. I was five years old and separated from my mother. Time was measured by when she'd come for me.

And finally, my mother did come back for me. As it happened, on that day, I didn't hear the knock on the door. It was just another ordinary day filled with the ordinary routines of orphanage life. Sister Maria tapped me on my shoulder and in her usual pleasant manner told me to follow her. We turned the corner from the hallway to the foyer.

I saw her. I stopped as if my feet had grown roots.

"Woon-hee yah. I am here," my mother said in her trilling voice. She came to me, bent down, and wrapped me in her arms. I stood rigid and mute, even though I wanted to shout angry words at her. My rapid heartbeat silenced my voice. I stayed in her arms until her warmth dispelled the loneliness and aching that had lodged in my heart for all those months.

"Are we going home, Omai?" I asked, with my face buried in her blouse.

"Yes. We are going home," she said as she picked me up and held me.

My mother's reference to "going home" meant going back to North Korea. She had decided we would return to North Korea where we had relatives. Aching from missing her children, she believed life would be less lonely there. We would all be together again. At least, she and I would be in the familiar surroundings of our village of Unryul.

We went to the boat dock. My mother found a boat scheduled to leave that day. We queued up. All the others in line were men. When my mother's turn came, she tried to book passage back to North Korea.

I became frightened when the man in charge started shouting at my mother.

"Woman, are you out of your mind?" he said. "Most people in North Korea are desperately trying to flee from there! And here you are—trying to go back?" He slapped my mother across her face and yelled, "Get out of here! Don't you ever try this again!" My mother's left hand flew to her face, protecting herself from the sting of his slap.

The ticket agent spat and shouted, "Next!"

I was terrified. I dared not cry. It would only have made matters worse for my mother. I held onto the folds of her skirt. When she stooped to pick up our blanket-wrapped bundle, I, too, leaned forward, still gripping her skirt.

My mother and I watched the boat leave the pier, heading for our homeland without us. In the ensuing days, weeks, months, and years, not a day passed without us remembering our life in our village of Unryul and yearning to return to the tranquility we had enjoyed there, before the division of our country.

We never discussed the incident on the boat dock, which changed the course of our lives. But such sensory and emotional imagery stays with one for a lifetime. I have often wondered how my life would have unfolded if that man had allowed my mother and me to board the boat back to North Korea. Years later, people are starving to death there. Newspapers are replete with photos of emaciated children, their heads and skeletal bodies out of proportion.

Satellite television flashes images of bent, weary women foraging for edible plants on barren mountains, while children search for scraps of firewood. For those people in North Korea, survival is a constant struggle. Would I have been one of those emaciated children? Would my mother have been one of those bent, weary women? Would we have survived?

What that ticket agent did seemed cruel to a five-year-old child. Fifty years later, looking back, what I see is a human being showing his capacity to care for other human beings. By barring us from boarding that boat to North Korea, he saved our lives, lives that would have been torn apart had it not been for that boat not taken.

HESITANT LIVES

Seoul, 1946

AFTER THE MAN SLAPPED my mother at the boat dock, my face stung as if I too had been slapped. I could still hear the cracking of his rough palm against my mother's soft cheek. I looked at Omai's face for signs. As if nothing out of the ordinary had happened, she bent down and lifted the large bundle wrapped in a blanket-sized cloth onto her head.

I asked, "Where are we going, Omai?"

"We are going to visit a halmoni (grandmother) from our village," my mother replied.

I looked up at her while firmly holding her hand. I wanted to send all the warmth in my heart through my grasp.

We boarded a taxi already crowded with people. We squeezed in the back, where I perched on the edge of the seat. Bodies packed together moved in waves as the taxi made turn after turn. We got out when we reached the city. My mother and I climbed to the top of a hill to this grandmother's house in Seoul. She welcomed us as if we were her kinfolk.

From that day on, like uprooted trees, we lived transplanted lives in a strange new city. From the tranquil, rural life of gentry to a life of chaotic, urban survival. From a double-gated residence to living quarters shared with others. From security to the unknown. We accepted unfamiliar acts, because we lived hesitant lives.

Refugees clung together in groups. Each group, based on the province from which it originated, formed a community. The elder members took the task of establishing the degrees of kinship among the families. They made certain everyone in the group was related.

Getting around Seoul required alertness. In our village, we strolled, but here we walked briskly, with grim determination. Most of the time, my mother carried me on her back, after my repeated falls from walking on uneven and pebbly ground. My skinned knees never had a chance to scab over. Each time we set forth, I anticipated a scary experience.

Four gates walled the city—north, south, east, and west. My mother and I would go to the South Gate market to buy our provisions. A child could get lost in the labyrinth. Stalls for produce, meat, fish, and poultry snaked through alleys, deep inside the gate. The meat section nauseated me. Large slabs of animal carcasses hung on iron hooks. Hens fluttering their feathers squawked in the meshed cages. From a thick meaty smell to the sharp stench of fish, it all overpowered my senses. I gagged.

My mother sometimes bought me an orange as a treat. That made the market day tolerable.

MY SECOND BROTHER HAD gone to live with distant relatives. When he returned, our small family of three moved in with a grandmother from our village. She lived with her granddaughter and grandson. Both families were without fathers. Whenever anyone asked me about the members of my family, I'd forget to include the elder of my brothers. Throughout my life, he remained a stranger to me. Sixteen years older than I, Big Brother lived at the university—which I thought was another city. He visited only occasionally.

Since Omai had neither a husband nor a mother-in-law to serve, she had an undefined role in this paternalistic country. So, she created her own. Unlike other women of her age and station in Korean society, she did not have the luxury of overseeing her household. During the day, she was away and I took her absence for granted. For her, it was a necessity.

I cannot explain how my mother managed to support us. Did her family in North Korea continue to send money? If so, how was that done? Perhaps some agreements were made among those left in the North and those who fled to the South.

I could only conjecture, from snippets of overheard conversations, what hardships my mother experienced. In the evening, I'd listen as she and the grandmother, our landlady, talked. Often, my mother explained why she could not pay the rent on time. She had not received the promissory note owed to her. The fact that someone promised money to my mother was beyond my comprehension. She talked in hushed tones about the black market. I gathered from whispers and shifting glances that they were not talking about the market at the South Gate. Although I never knew for certain, I believed she stretched her meager allotment by working her money in the black market.

Years later, when I was traveling abroad, a woman of my mother's age came up to me and asked, in accented, memorized English, "Change money?" She could eke out a small profit by illegally changing my U.S. dollars into her country's currency. Watching her, I flashed on an image of my own mother. Did she utter these same words? My lips mouthed the word "no" to the foreign woman but my heart was beating "yes."

My mother's days started early. She walked to the various government locations and lined up with the rest of the gathered crowd for coupons and rations of rice. She sold portions of the rationed products to those who could afford to buy. Those were years when the country struggled to recover from nearly four decades of Japanese occupation. Just like my knees, there was no time to heal. The country now faced the aftermath of World War II, a pawn in a power game between the Russians and the Americans.

Our temporary stay with this grandmother lasted four years. Then one day, the house shook when the sky exploded and bombs rained down.

FRIENDLY BOMBS

Seoul, 1950

IT WAS JUNE 1950 in Seoul, Korea. The world labeled it the start of the Korean Conflict. Innocent people died, and hopes and dreams evaporated with the dropping of bombs. I don't know why this atrocity was called a conflict. It was war.

I was nine years old when it began. One day, life was normal. Overnight, everything changed. I can best describe those days in terms of opposites: satiety and hunger, safety and danger, home and homeless, war and peace, life and death. Communist North Korea launched a blitzkrieg against South Korea. The North Korean troops took Seoul, the capital of South Korea, in three days. Bombs destroyed our homes.

In the days before June 25, 1950, my friend, Myung Ja, who lived on the same street, would come early and knock on my door. We had finished third grade that year. The entire summer was ours to do with as we pleased.

We never had any trouble finding things to amuse us. For playing house, I had the best collection of dishes. My mother had taken broken china and grated the sharp edges against a large rock until the edges were as smooth as my cheek. Sometimes, the friction from the porcelain grinding against the rock created a burning smell as if it were on fire.

When we got tired of playing house, we'd take off to roam the streets. It didn't take long for us to find other companions. One day, we played soldiers with the neighborhood boys. Another time, we caught dragonflies. On a dare, I ate one.

On June 25, Myung Ja did not knock on my door. That day the Communist North Korean troops launched the attack across the 38th parallel. All adult conversations centered on the mass hysteria over the Reds' (the Communists') invasion. We were to flee from our homes. We had no doubt evil Reds would kill us all.

Soon my family moved to a makeshift shelter.

In the middle of the night, Communist soldiers raided our makeshift dwellings. The soldiers burst into the common room, scanning the place with their rifles. They saw groups of women and young children huddled together. All of us remained silent. Only the babies cooed. When a baby cried, the mother would stifle the noise by thrusting her breast into the baby's mouth. The soldiers strutted around the room.

"Where are your husbands and sons?" the soldier with the most stripes on his uniform bellowed. They were searching for men and older boys to conscript into the Communist army.

"We are so sorry, but as you can see, we only have women and children here," an old grandmother answered.

"Isn't this something! Bo gee dul man sah rah (Only the vaginas live here)," the officer said. He ordered his men to search the premises. I closed my eyes. I could visualize my seventeen-year-old brother lying flat on his back on a false ceiling in the attic, the space so small that his nose touched the actual ceiling. I quickly erased that thought, fearing that the soldiers could read my mind.

Finding no males, the soldiers corralled the women and children at gunpoint. Only the elderly and nursing mothers were allowed to remain at the shelter. My mother and I were among the able-bodied women and children. At the officer's order, soldiers shoved us into the back of the army truck. Seated on the floor, I pressed my body close to Omai. I was scared, but I was old enough to keep quiet and remain alert. The ride seemed long on the bumpy roads. No one spoke, not even the watchful soldiers. Our collective bodies swayed as the truck took the turns. Finally, the truck screeched to a stop. By the time we reached our destination, night had fallen. In the darkness, the only things I saw were buildings. We were at a secret munitions yard. My mother and I were assigned to transport bombs from the yard into surrounding buildings, a covert task that took place only at night. Even the soldiers who ordered us spoke in hushed yet urgent tones. I followed my mother in the dark.

Mounds of stacked bombs were to be moved into the buildings. When my mother stooped to pick up a bomb, I bent to lift the other end. The guard blocked me and said, "One bomb, one person." He pulled me by my arm away from my mother. I obeyed. I struggled and strained to lift each bomb. They were heavy for an emaciated girl weighing less than sixty pounds. I carried each bomb in my arms and walked with short strides as fast as I could. After depositing a bomb onto the growing stack, I tried to slow my pace back to the arsenal while looking furtively for shadowy figures monitoring us.

This went on for several months, and Omai was not happy that her little daughter had to carry bombs. When the moon looked like a silver-slivered eyebrow and did not illuminate the arsenal, she took my hand and hid me in a dark place until the labor ended. We learned to communicate with each other without words, just with our eyes and hearts. I knew from the expression on her face and her gestures, that were also my gestures, what she was thinking and feeling. It would always be that way: throughout our life together, I would always be an extension of my mother, her gong-dai, her tail.

By August 1950, the Communists had invaded all of South Korea except for the southern port city of Pusan. Under United Nations auspices, the United States intervened. Helpless civilians were caught in the crossfire.

We were trapped in occupied Seoul. The only place of refuge and solace during this war was the Myeondong Cathedral. Coming back from Mass one day, I was thrilled to see the thundering fighter airplanes painted with American flags, as I had heard the adults whisper that the Yankees were gaining ground. Bombs dropped from our Yankee friends' planes, along with thousands of pieces of paper imprinted with General Douglas MacArthur's photo. The sky was littered with floating white paper leaves. I was told the bombs were friendly bombs, but the bombs did not discriminate. They killed friends and foes, enemies and innocent people.

Subterranean walkways, packed with corpses, served as tombs for the dead and the living. Babies too young to walk sat crying next to dead mothers whose arms still clung to them. We took the underground tunnel, a shortcut from the cathedral to our shelter. As we made our way, I gripped my mother's hand and closed my eyes to shut out the horror. My mother led me, as if I were blinded by the sights we were walking through. To this day, these are images I cannot erase.

THE PLUM VENDOR

AFTER WE LEFT THE temporary shelter, we moved to a community facility where my mother cooked in exchange for our lodging. On days she was off, she left at dawn and walked many miles to pick plums in the countryside. When she had picked as many as she could fit into her bamboo basket, she twined a towel into a circular mat to go underneath it, crouched down, keeping her upper body erect, and someone would help her lift her heavy load onto her head. In the intense heat of summer, she trekked the long distance to the city on dirt roads.

Each morning, my mother left me a small earthen bowl of barley rice. My job was to set up a straw mat on a busy market street and sell the plums. As the day wore on, my hunger intensified. Realizing that the bowl of rice was the sole sustenance for both of us, I ate one chopstick of rice. Chewing slowly to savor the taste, I hoped if I took my time eating, I would feel satiated. I thought of my mother picking plums and replaced the lid on the bowl so as not to be tempted. When my stomach growled and hurt with spasms, I took several more grains of rice.

Some days, I left my mother less than half a bowl.

One day, excitement stirred through the compound where we lived with the other displaced families. I didn't know why because the adults tried their best to shield the children from many atypical, yet necessary, acts during these desperate times. The word spread that someone had killed a dog, meaning there would be meat to eat for a change.

The adults, huddled together, planned and then prepared the meal. All the preparation was done out of sight. Only the pungent smell of cooking flesh penetrated the shelter. When cooked, the meat was divided up. My mother brought me a piece. As much as I wanted to eat it, I could not. I was not hungry enough, not starving enough, to devour that piece of dog meat.

Not yet.

One day, while I was selling plums, a girl about my age put her mat down next to mine. I wanted to be the sole plum vendor, and she was muscling into my business. I sized up the intruder. I knew by looking her over that she had to be what my mother described as coming from the peasant stock, not the Yangban (upper class), like our family. Her tanned, round face, piano legs, and large feet meant that she and her family were laborers, not scholars like mine.

She copied whatever I did. I polished my plums and arranged them in neat rows. She did the same. There was no way of hiding my sales secrets from her. Over the days, however, I discovered that she was lazy. She did not go out of her way to sell her plums, and at the end of every day, I always sold far more than she. I was proud of my sales skills and my plums.

Some days, without notice, the official "comrades" interrupted our business by ordering the girl and me to attend a class. They took us to a building where around twenty children of all sizes were corralled in a large room. First, the adult leader led us in singing the National Anthem of North Korea. He sang so loudly he did not know that the assembled children made random sounds instead. I don't recall the specific indoctrination lectures, as I had many worries on my mind. The leader led us in doing physical exercises. I had no underwear. My skirt was all I wore. I worried about how to jump and bend without exposing myself. Throughout that time, I was thinking about my plums. What if someone stole them? I wanted to get back to my plums.

Later, I found out I didn't need to worry so much. When I told my mother about my day spent learning communist propaganda, she said, "All the money we make from selling the plums is divided equally among the plum vendors. That is what communism is, equality for all." After that, I did not feel so happy about working hard to sell more plums than my neighbor.

VISIT WITH AN
ENEMY SOLDIER

Seoul, July 1950

ONE DAY, THERE WAS a knock at our door. My mother opened it as I peered out from behind her. A soldier no more than twelve years old asked in a familiar dialect, "Ajummoni, please give me some water." He sounded just like my cousin in our hometown of Unryul.

My mother obliged, but watched him carefully. He took the glass and drank in one long gulp, thanked her, and left. She locked the door after him. Like the glass the boy handed back, my mother was empty of her usual hospitality. That was when I realized that she did not see a lad from her province, but an enemy soldier—until one hot July day.

My mother and I walked across the city to a huge building. It could have been a school converted into a headquarters for the occupying North Korean armed forces. When we entered the reception area, my mother said, "I am going to work at the commissary today. I want you to sit quietly in that corner." She pointed to an out-of-the-way spot.

I sensed her serious mood. I knew that in times of danger, she would sometimes leave me in order to protect me. This must be one of those days, I thought. There were several folding chairs haphazardly placed. I positioned one in the corner where I could easily track her.

The reception area led to a large auditorium that served as the commissary. The North Korean officers strutted in and out. They addressed all the workers as "comrades," including my mother. Seeing how she had to wait on them with bowed head, serving food with both hands, it seemed to me that she was more a servant than a comrade.

The officers were seated in groups at long tables. Some were busily shoveling food into their mouths with chopsticks, others were leisurely drinking and chatting. I was mesmerized by one officer who sat alone with one leg crossed over the other, blowing out circular rings from his cigarette. These fluid white circles floated and dissipated. The scene had a mute yet lyrical air.

I focused my attention on my mother. Her routine became repetitive from my vantage point. She'd clear the dishes and wipe the tables. When a new customer entered, she'd bow her welcome and lead the officer to a table. I could predict her movements. Abruptly, this pace of her routine elasticized into slow motion. She stopped wiping the table. She clutched the rag and stared across the room. I followed her gaze. There stood a tall man in an officer's uniform.

He walked toward her. She straightened and wiped her hands on her apron, her eyes still fixed on him. Then they stood facing one other, a North Korean army officer and my mother. They did not smile, but their lips moved.

Time stopped. My stomach somersaulted. I feared for her safety. He walked away and she watched him go. Then she took her rag out of her apron pocket and went back to cleaning the littered tables.

When her shift ended, we walked hand in hand in the sunset to our shelter. I asked, "Who was that tall man you spoke to today?"

"That man is my youngest brother, your uncle. You don't remember him, do you?"

The news stunned me.

Omai explained, "Some people from our province arranged our meeting. I kept it from you because it could have been a dangerous situation. For both him and me."

"What did he say?" I wanted to know.

"He told me that my mother is well. That my father passed away. He said that he joined the army so that he can provide for his family. He told me not to worry about our family in North Korea. He will take good care of them. He said for us to remain in South Korea and one day we will see each other again."

Still holding hands, I lagged behind a few steps to keep from tripping on the uneven pavement. My mother slowed her pace and looked at me.

"Did I tell you I raised him when he was a baby?" Without waiting for my reply, she uttered, "I didn't even get to touch his hand."

I tightened my grasp of her hand.

That visit with her brother was to be the last she saw of him.

THE TRAIN TO PUSAN

Two months into the war, my mother and I lived in temporary shelters. Our roommates were fellow war refugees. Every evening, Omai and I staked out a corner of the large rooms we stayed in. I helped my mother spread out our one bedroll. Then all the women gathered and visited, but their hands were never idle while they talked. Some cleaned, some mended clothes, and some prepared food.

The newest problem was lice. My hair teemed with them. Omai would sit me down between her legs and pick out one louse at a time. She squashed each between her thumbnails. Black blood splattered her fingers. Then she scratched the snowy nits off my scalp.

One woman had a system for mass louse annihilation. She discovered that they liked to live in the seams of clothes, so she took her family's clothing and ran her teeth along the seams, chomping chatter-like from one end to the other. I imagined crushed lice in cloth catacombs.

Combatting lice was an evening task. The first morning task was to pry my eyes open. They were so infected from the unsanitary conditions that I saw through a gray haze of pus. Overnight, the buildup dried and glued my eyes shut. I had no eyelashes left. Every morning, Omai used a bowl of water previously boiled and cooled to clean my eyes.

One morning, Omai woke me earlier than usual. "We have to hurry," she whispered as she cleaned my eyes. "Piran ga yeh deh."

"What is piran?" I asked.

"We have to flee from here. The Reds are gaining ground. It is no longer safe for us in Seoul." Her movements were quick as she collected our belongings. "Get dressed. We leave soon for the train depot."

CROWDS MILLED AROUND THE railroad station, pandemonium everywhere. I held onto Omai's free hand. With her other hand, she balanced a large bundle of our possessions on her head. She led us toward a monstrous black locomotive fuming on its track. Men shouted orders to whoever would obey. Old people shuffled about as fast as they could. Some children like me were quiet. Others were boisterous. The babies were tied securely to their mothers' backs with a ddee, a long blanket belt. The front railroad cars were already packed with people. We hurried and made our way to a car toward the rear of the train.

"Ajummoni, come over here," shouted a man younger than Omai. He helped her with her bundle as she climbed aboard. Then he hoisted me up beside her. The boxcar filled up fast. We moved to one side. Each family huddled together as more people were shoved into our already packed car.

With the exception of the aged who sat on their family's possessions, most of us stood. The large railcar did not have any chairs or benches. I felt suffocated, standing with my face pressing against people's chests or backs. I felt the heartbeats of those around me. The stench of sweat and urine stung my nose. I panted, breathing through my mouth.

The train jerked forward, the lurching conveyed to all the cars. The only air and light came from the open door of the boxcar. I peered out between people as the train chugged along. My cloudy vision painted the passing scenery a fuzzy gray, a blur of gable-roofed houses, farms with thatch-roofed huts, and orchards and oxen plowing fields.

With a shrill blast of its whistle, the train entered a tunnel. Eyes wide open, I experienced an empty blackness. The dark magnified the noise of the train and the smell of the surrounding bodies. The train clattered on and on.

Finally, it stopped.

Outside, vendors on a train platform were selling their wares. "Ne bae sa seh yo (Buy my pears)," a man with a basket of fruit called out.

"Bae" means both pears and stomach. I knew we didn't have any money to buy a pear. He might as well have been selling his stomach. His Southern dialect sounded strange.

"Where are we?" I asked my mother. "Why do these people speak so funny?"

"We are in Taegu. Halfway to Pusan, our destination."

WHEN WE GOT OFF the train, I pulled on Omai's skirt. "Omai, ozum nuh ya deh!" I said, as I squeezed my legs together to forestall the need to urinate.

Omai looked around. With lifted skirt, an old woman squatted on the dirt bank beyond the platform, urinating. My mother took my hand and led me over to her.

"I can't go here," I cried as drops slid down my legs.

Omai took off her outer skirt and shielded me from the others.

"But they'll know what I am doing."

"Go," Omai said. I did not even have a chance to squat. A river of ojum snaked a path on the ground. My legs splattered with urine.

We headed back. Omai saw water trickling out from underneath the train. Water! She crouched down and cupped her hands under the escaping water. Suddenly, a blast of white steam spurted from the spout and scalded her outstretched hands and arms. She reeled back.

"Omai!" I shouted.

That steam signaled that the train was about to leave again. We scrambled aboard. Others examined my mother's burns and clucked their tongues in sympathy. They made room for us to sit on our bundle. Her scalded skin peeled off like old, flimsy paper, and the raw flesh oozed. No one had any salve to protect and soothe her injury. I shivered as if my own hands and arms were sliced by a thousand paper cuts.

We sat side by side on the reverberating bundle.

"You have so much pus in your eyes," my mother said. "Can you see anything?"

"Everything is blurry, Omai, but my eyes don't hurt." I blinked hard trying to get rid of the sticky substance. Each time I did, it stretched across my eyes like rubber bands.

"Woon-hee yah," Omai said. "Look up."

I tilted my head back and opened my eyes as wide as I could. I felt her breath on my face. She thrust her tongue into my right eye and licked it clean. Without a word, she did the same to my left one. The warmth and softness of her tongue caressed me, even when her burnt hands could not.

THE LOCOMOTIVE, DRAGGING DILAPIDATED boxcars full of refugees, arrived in Pusan on a gloomy morning. It belched out its dirty, exhausted passengers.

"Now what, Omai?" I asked my mother.

REFUGEE LIFE

Pusan, 1950

A LONG WITH OTHER REFUGEES, my mother and I lived in a churchyard. Crudely made tents of assorted sizes and shapes dotted the entire ground. Ours had enough space to spread out our bedroll and for a chamber pot. In front of the opening of the tent, my mother devised a cooking pit. She arranged rocks to serve as a circular border for the pit. My job was to help gather the wood for the fire.

I watched her rub two stones vigorously until they sparked. The first time I saw this, I thought it was magic. Every evening, that was how she started the fire to cook our one meal of rice gruel.

After a while, life in the churchyard had a rhythm. During the day, only old people and young children remained at the yard. We children were left to our own devices, as the adults were preoccupied with the urgent business of survival.

Because the country was at war, there were no schools. One day, a teacher assembled us children from the churchyard and started her own school. Each morning, she lined us up by the church gate, the shortest to the tallest. We followed her to our outdoor school, a space in a corner of the churchyard. On some days, we took a field trip to the nearby hill, my favorite spot. Trees greeted us with their fresh woodsy smell. When we sang, I swallowed the fragrance whenever I took a breath.

We had no books, paper, or pencils, but our teacher taught us to read and write and to compute. We had to wait until the wood from the cooking fire turned into charcoal. With a small, charred stick, I practiced my penmanship and did my lessons on the pavement of the churchyard.

I do not remember my teacher's name. I cannot recall her face. But what is etched in my memory is her generous gift, her teaching.

I REMEMBER THE FIRST time I met Yankee soldiers while playing near the churchyard. They looked so different from us. Some had eyes the color of sky and hair the color of straw. I wondered, "Can they see with those eyes?" And staring at those big noses, I guessed that they could smell a lot.

Three Yankee soldiers approached. They spoke in their language, uttering sounds I could not pronounce. The boys in our group mimicked the tongue-twisting sounds. The soldiers laughed. I was too shy to try.

One soldier became my favorite Yankee. He blew up a balloon for each of us. He huffed and puffed until his pale, freckled face turned pink. Our own mouths breathed in sync. That wonderful day we marched back to our churchyard holding identical white, elliptical balloons. The soldier had given me the fattest and longest balloon.

The soldiers also gave each of us something wrapped in green paper. They showed us how to eat the flat food by removing the paper cover and then slowly opening the shiny silver paper. They popped the thin rectangular object I didn't recognize as food into their mouths and chewed with gusto. The more adventurous boys followed the soldiers' examples. Not me. I put mine away inside my pocket.

That night, I took out the item and showed it to my mother.

"Omai, the Yankee soldier put this in his mouth," I reported.

"Let me see," she said. She unwrapped the green paper and then the silver paper. She examined the contents.

"It looks like go-moo," she said.

"Rubber, is it? Try it, Omai," I exclaimed.

She stuck the thin, flat piece in her mouth and chewed.

"How does it taste?" I asked. She took it out of her mouth—a little ball! Smiling, she placed it in my mouth. Go-moo was still sweet. From that day on, it was our ritual—my mother would thaw the go-moo in preparation for my own sweet pleasure.

IN THE TWILIGHT, THE adults in the nearby tents would gather and discuss the progression of the war. By August 1950, the North Korean troops occupied all but what was labeled as the Pusan perimeter, bordered on the west by the Naktong River. Only a fifty-mile plot of the land was left for North Korea to seize.

The news grew increasingly dire. On the evening of August 31, 1950, North Korean Infantry divisions, twenty thousand men strong, crossed the east bank of the Naktong River. They were more than a match for the receding armed forces of South Korea and the United States.

I wondered if my Yankee soldier had survived. I could see him in my mind, the soldier with blue eyes and yellow hair who had given me two packs of chewing gum and the fattest balloon. Wars are cruel. Yet small acts of kindness occur even in the chaos. It took me a half a century to realize this—a longer time than it took me to distinguish a condom from a balloon.

GOING TO MI-GOOK

IN THE MIDST OF the full-blown war, as the North Korean army, aided by the Chinese, charged south toward Pusan, my mother managed to get us out of Korea. In the fall of 1951, we left our native country for Mi-Gook (Beautiful Land)—America.

Our escape began one day when we were sheltering in Pusan as refugees. My mother and I went to see a man in his office in a tall building. When we entered, he came over to us. "Ajummoni, how are you?" he asked, bowing to her. My mother bowed in return. He looked at me and said, "This must be your daughter." He motioned for us to sit in the two chairs facing his desk.

After we settled, he went to his chair and sat. On his desk sat stacks of papers. On the wall behind him were posters of bridges, ships, airplanes. I did not know it then, but we were at a government travel department.

He was a young man, about Big Brother's age. He reviewed many documents with my mother. She listened and nodded in acknowledgment. Our meeting took a long time. I watched him methodically insert a carbon paper between two papers, one set after another. When the final document was stamped with the do-jahng (signature stamp), he compiled all the papers. As we stood to leave, the man gave me a tag imprinted with a shiny silver-colored airplane. I ran my hand across the sticker, feeling the outline of the airplane. I asked my mother, "Are we going to go on an airplane like this one?" She replied, "We will fly on an airplane to Japan and from there we will go to Mi-Gook by ship."

MY MOTHER AND I left Korea in the middle of a raging war. We left behind the blaring sirens and exploding bombs that had punctuated our existence. We left with only one black cardboard suitcase; I had stuck my silver airplane tag right in the center of one side of it. I wore the myung-jil, the holiday garment my mother had made for Lunar New Year's Day the year of the war. In ordinary circumstances, I could have been dressed like this for a party. Instead, we boarded an airplane with noisy propellers. Neither of us had flown before.

I sat in the window seat, not knowing what to expect. I paid attention and stayed glued to my mother, mirroring everything she did, even folding my hands on my lap. I was safe as long as I was with her. After the takeoff, I peered out the window. Buildings became specks as we ascended higher and higher, and soon the airplane passed into cottony clouds. I held my breath so I wouldn't get smothered.

When we landed in Japan, it was raining. Foreign land, foreign people, foreign speech. A Japanese mother and her daughter caught my attention. They wore kimonos and wooden platform shoes. Under their shared umbrella, they were smiling, oblivious to their surroundings. That little girl had her hair in two ponytails tied with red ribbons.

I wanted ribbons like hers. My mother and I, in our Korean garments and our gomoo shin (traditional boat-shaped rubber shoes), were the foreigners. Our short blouses and billowy full skirts contrasted with the Japanese tight-fitting gown cinched with an obi at the waist. At that moment, I wanted to be that Japanese girl with red bow ties in her hair.

WHILE I FELT LIKE an outsider, my mother seemed at ease with the ways of the Japanese. I did not know then that she was only five years old when Japan began the occupation of Korea. Much to my surprise, she spoke fluent Japanese.

The port city of Yokohama, our gateway to Mi-Gook, was much bigger than Inchon. We crossed railroad tracks to get to the shipyard. Each mode of transportation competed to make the loudest noise. The trains whistled in sustained high pitches, trucks took turns honking, and the ships blew their horns in bass, as if to notify others of their importance.

We found our ship. It was huge, with a black hull and white trim at the top, and a shiny black smokestack. It was named after an American president—President Wilson, perhaps. Knowing the name would not have made any difference for my mother and me. The ship was magnificent. I looked up at the tiny figures already on board, waving at us.

There were four of us cramped in a cabin that consisted of two bunk beds on each side, with a narrow aisle in the middle. At the end of the cabin was a tiny bathroom that only one person could fit into at a time. The first time we peeked in the restroom and saw a round bowl containing water, I asked my mother, "What is this?" She turned the faucets on in the sink and then turned them off. Thinking out loud, she said, "Since this bowl is the sink, that must be the ship's version of a toilet." Having said that, she hopped onto the rim of the toilet bowl, perching her feet on it and demonstrated the position by squatting.

The other passengers in the cabin were two young Korean women. The older of the two was a quiet person who kept to herself—as much as that was possible in a room so small. She sat on the edge of her bed and read.

The younger woman was around nineteen or twenty. She was the lively one. I observed her each morning, getting ready for the day. She smeared Pond's Cold Cream on her face, then used her handkerchief to wipe off the shine. Next, she opened a round container and dipped a small pad in the white powder inside, which she patted onto her face. The bottom of the box had English letters, COTY. That was another object I desired.

The younger woman was our intermediary to anything outside of our cabin. That might explain an exciting and disturbing incident in our cabin one night.

On our side, my mother slept on the bottom bed and I on the top. On the other side, the older woman slept on the bottom and the younger one on the upper bunk. That night, when asleep, I sensed a rustle. I opened my eyes. In the dark, I could see someone moving. From the upper bunk, the young woman shouted, "There's a man in our cabin!" All three of us sat up.

"Who is there?" My mother's voice rang out.

A dark figure headed for the cabin door. Outside light beamed in as he slipped out, and the door shut before my mother could apprehend him. The young woman was sobbing and crying out, "Aiyee, Omoni," calling for her mother.

There was no way any of us could go back to sleep. The girl told us the intruder was a cabin steward. She dramatically enacted his groping and her struggle to get free from his embrace. She was able to calm down then.

Her story enthralled me. But I could tell by the frown on my mother's face and by her "tsk, tsk" clucking, she was disturbed. Yet, no one reported the incident. After that, my mother made sure that we locked the door and wedged a chair in front of it for extra security.

FOR THE FIRST SEVERAL days, I was seasick and could not keep any food down. The ship's rule dictated that children ate at an earlier time than adults. My mother had the company of the two other cabinmates at mealtime, but I was alone at meals. For three days, my mother brought back a little rice and pickled radish (daikon) for me. When I finally joined the children at the dining table set for eight, the other children ordered their meals. They all spoke English, even some children who did not look like Yankees. I just sat there. Each day, the waiter brought me food identical to what the younger girl sitting next to me ordered. I could only pick at it. After over a year of near starvation, I could not eat rich food laced with creamy sauces; my stomach could not tolerate it. I just wanted familiar food: rice and kimchi.

THE FIRST TIME I saw the Pacific Ocean, on which our ship sailed, my mother called the vast ocean "Tae-Pyung." I asked what that name meant. "Peaceful," she said. The Pacific Ocean was such a contrast from the war zone we left behind.

During the journey, I whiled away the time on the ship's deck. The blue ocean stretched across the horizon to meet the sky. Only a faint line of a different shade of blue divided the sky from the water. Sometimes, I'd lie on my back and look up at my own private art gallery in the sky. Clouds of different shapes and sizes depicted an assemblage of animals. My celestial zoo kept me company throughout the voyage.

The days passed. How many of them, I don't know. Two weeks? Three weeks? Then one day, we saw land. My mother told me that the ship would be stopping at an island called Hawaii. I asked her, "What is an island?"

"Sohm is land surrounded by water," she explained.

Since Yokohama, we had seen no land until our ship docked in Honolulu. We were stopping there for a day. Our cabin companion, the quiet, older one, had church connections there, and she invited us to tour the island with her and her friends. The pastor and two parishioners met us at the port and we rode in the pastor's car around the island stopping at vista points. I saw rows of tall trees unlike any I had ever seen before. These trees had no branches; they had straight, long trunks topped with crowns of bladelike leaves. I also saw brown-skinned people for the first time.

Everything was so bright, I had to squint. The sunlight tinted the color of water to emerald green. My mother leaned over and said, "Cham jochi?" I answered, "Yes, it is very nice." That brief ride around the island was the first and only time we were together in Honolulu. Throughout the years later, she and I often spoke of returning to Honolulu, but everyday life intruded.

The Pacific Ocean became its namesake when the ocean liner glided under the Golden Gate Bridge one sunny morning in October 1951. We had come to America, the Beautiful Land.

PART 2

IMMIGRANTS IN AMERICA

PLACES CALLED HOME

Los Angeles, 1951

"I COME FROM ALABAMA with a banjo on my knee," my mother liked to sing.

She and I came from Korea with a black cardboard suitcase.

One October morning in 1951, we stood in front of a large two-story house on Ellendale Place in Los Angeles. Above the entrance, a sign in Korean assured us that we had located what we were looking for: the Korean Senior Center. Omai put our suitcase down and rang the doorbell. A Korean woman opened the huge door and invited us in. We took off our shoes and entered.

A prominent staircase spiraled up to the second floor. To the right was the salon with a fireplace. A diminutive Korean man in a blue suit rushed out and greeted my mother. The host led us into the salon where four aged men sat. They appeared glad to have a diversion. A spry man stood and exchanged bows with Omai. The others struggled to scoot to the edge of their chairs when Omai went to them and uttered, "Ahn young hah se yo? (How are you?)" They bowed their heads and returned the greeting. I copied Omai and bowed and then noticed Omai and I were the only ones without shoes. I curled my toes to make my feet invisible.

Omai addressed the man in the suit. "We are here about a place to live. Is it still available?"

"Yes. Please sit down. But it's not what I'm sure you're used to."

The woman who had answered the doorbell came in with a tray full of cups and handed them out to all the men in the room. "Please have a cup of coppee," she said as she offered one to my mother.

Omai took it and thanked the woman. Politeness ruled. In Korean, coppee means nosebleed. She held the cup with both hands without drinking.

I looked around the salon: two identical beige velvet sofas faced one another, with the large wooden coffee table in between, and four beige wingback chairs were placed near the bay window, which faced the street. A beautiful objet d'art stood on the mantel of the fireplace. Were we to live with these old men?

The man in the suit set his cup on the coffee table, slapped his knees, rose to his full five feet and said, "Let me show you the place."

We followed our host down a hall and out the back door. He led us to one of two sheds in the yard. The door creaked as he opened it. "This room can be used for cooking and eating," he said, as he pointed out the shed's features. Beside a deep washbasin, an electric coil hot plate with two cooking surfaces perched on a worn card table. Two metal folding chairs leaned against a wall. A faded yellow couch hinted at a living room.

A partition that stopped short of touching one side of the wall divided the rectangular shed in two. The gap served as a doorway into another room that contained a brass bed with four tall bedposts. The bed filled the room from wall to wall and from ceiling to floor. I couldn't take my eyes off this large regal bed. It looked like the bed I'd seen in an illustration in a book I'd read before the war—a story about a princess and a pea.

Omai searched beyond the bedroom. "Where is the toilet facility?" she asked.

"Ah, you have to go into the main house for that," he said. "This was not made for housing purposes when it was built."

"Is that so?" my mother said. "Har su up suh yo (It cannot be helped)," she continued, talking to herself. I had heard Omai utter those words whenever there were no more options. "We will take it," she declared.

We moved in with our one cardboard suitcase. We kept to ourselves, for the most part, except when we needed to use the restroom. I, however, made friends with an old man who resided in the big house. Or rather, he made me his friend. Each morning, when I crept into the house to use the toilet, my friend appeared out of nowhere and offered me candy from the palm of his hand. I wondered if he had been taller in his younger years and shrunk with age. He and I were at eye level with each other.

"Did you sleep well, Harabuji (Grandfather)?" I inquired, offering the traditional morning greeting.

"Pretty girl, would you like some candy?" he asked.

I took my time eyeing the assortment of candies, picked one for the day, and thanked him. That was a time of innocence when a lonely old man could reach out to a young girl as a granddaughter he never had. He seemed to appreciate our ritual as much as I did—maybe more.

EIGHT O'CLOCK SATURDAY EVENINGS were reserved for our weekly bath in the upstairs bathroom of the main house. The entire process took an hour. First, we had to remember to take everything we needed. Omai made sure we looked presentable as we passed by the other residents and exchanged pleasantries as though we were on a stroll.

The claw-foot tub was deep. After a thorough scrub, Omai filled the tub with hot water, so that steam rose from it. The mirror fogged over and the air became heavy with moisture. We immersed our bodies slowly so we could withstand the heat. Omai reclined on the end with the faucet, I on the curved end. We soaked to loosen any accumulated dirt. Omai scrubbed my back, then I washed hers, being careful to avoid her pea-sized brown mole.

We drained the dirty water, then cleaned the ring of scum, before refilling the tub with clean water. After rinsing off, we toweled our bodies, our skin pink from the scrubbing and the scalding water.

Our Saturday evening ritual was our version of the public bathhouses we had frequented in Korea before the war. There, my mother and I would walk to the neighborhood bathhouse. At the entrance, she would line up and pay the fees. The huge facility was divided so that men and women had their own bathhouses. Young children usually went with the women. The entire procedure from initial rinse outside of the communal tub to final rinse took an hour, like our private baths. I remember how light I felt afterward because of all the dirt my mother had scraped off my skin with her scrub cloth.

As we had in the old country after our bath, we walked with the moonlight illuminating our path. My mother sang a song about the moon watching over us wherever we might be: "Dah ra, dah ra, barl gun dah ra . . . (Moon, oh, moon, you bright moon . . . on you grows a laurel tree.)" For a moment, I forgot we were a continent and a vast ocean away from home.

I WAS CURIOUS ABOUT the shed next to ours. One day, I went inside. Cartons filled with used clothes and other assorted items sat haphazardly on the concrete floor. Bigger items like lamps and chairs were stacked in a corner. I took a mental inventory of all the goods and rushed back to report to my mother. We soon found out that this shed housed donated goods for a charity in Korea, and we were given permission to have first pick of the discarded items.

We scurried to the shed, opened the dusty boxes, and dug in.

"American ladies are big," I said as I held up a dress.

Omai slipped her small foot into a boat of a shoe. "They have large feet, too," she said.

I found a dress that might fit her. While she tried it on, I stood watch at the window. Those old men, with nothing to do, seemed to pop up anytime and anywhere.

"How do I look?" she asked.

I turned to see and bent over laughing. In the frilly, rose-patterned dress with puffed sleeves she looked ridiculous. "Omai!" I managed to say between squeals of laughter. She glanced down at herself and burst out laughing, too.

The boxes didn't hold as many girls' clothes. Omai found a jacket and matching pants in purple and green plaid. She examined them and declared they were in good condition. Although they were too big for me, we took them anyway. "In another year they will fit you fine," she said. That was a fruitful day. Two dresses, one pair of ladies' shoes, one pair of the smallest size men's shoes, and my future garments. And a coat for Omai.

Omai always used the restroom before dawn. In November, the weather turned cold. One morning she donned the black fur coat we had retrieved from the storage shed and went into the main house in the dark. Screams! A man's followed by my mother's. She rushed back to our shed.

"What's the matter, Omai?" I was sitting up in bed by now.

"Ne ga hone na suh! (I was frightened!) That old man came out of nowhere and started shouting, 'Aigoo, aigoo.'" She leaned on the wall, trying to calm herself.

She had scared my old friend, the candy man, who had thought she was an urban black bear on a prowl. She returned the fur coat to the charity bin.

SIX WEEKS INTO OUR new American life, the leaves on the tall mulberry tree in the backyard turned shades of yellow and golden brown, just like in the old country. My mother reminisced about how her family had grown silkworms when she was a young girl. She had climbed mulberry trees to pick the tender young leaves for their silkworms. Her mother's silk was the finest in town. One skein of it had come to America with us in that cardboard suitcase. Whenever she talked about her mother, she'd look beyond the horizon and utter, "Neh gahsum ee suri suri han da. (My heart is rubbed raw.)" I didn't know the words "suri suri" then, but I understood their meaning from my mother's expression. All the longing and aching of her heart were written on her face.

One day, the housekeeper knocked on our door. We invited her in. "This Thursday is Thanksgiving," she said. "Please join us for Thanksgiving dinner. We are serving tuh-kee."

I glanced at my mother. She read my thoughts. Tuh-kee sounded like toki—"rabbit."

"Thank you so much for your generous invitation but please excuse us. We do not eat toki," my mother replied.

I waited for a reaction. The housekeeper smiled a know-ing smile and replied, "No, we are not going to eat a rabbit. Tuh-kee is an American word for a large fowl."

To save face, my mother lamented how hampered she was for not being able to speak English. We then had our first Thanksgiving dinner in America. Turkey, rice, and kimchi.

MANY FULL MOONS LATER, when I was eleven years old, we moved from the carriage shed to a house behind Luckey's department store on Vermont and Jefferson. Our new house was an upgrade with its indoor toilet, stove, and icebox. It even had a strip of dirt yard in the back.

A paint-peeled shack, the rooms were tiny: the bedroom and bathroom on the right, the living room and kitchen on the left of a narrow hallway. At the rear of the house, a sliver of a porch enclosed by ripped, opaque plastic masqueraded as another room. A dirt patch separated this property from the next house. At the edge of the property, a dilapidated, splintered wooden fence stood like a row of loose teeth. At one blow, the fence could have collapsed.

Although our house itself was run-down, our front "yard"—the back parking lot for Luckey's—was urban with a capital U. Cars zoomed by day and night. The Vermont trolley was still operating; later, the roar of buses replaced the clanging of the trolley bells. Often sirens of all sorts blared. The city was alive.

I'd sit by the window in the front room for hours and watch people. I had my own peep show. One of the most exciting sights was Mr. Luckey and a woman in his car.

GOING OUT OF BUSINESS was painted in red, blue, and white on the front windows of Luckey's store. Mr.

Luckey may have been in his thirties or forties. I was not a good judge of age of the Bak-In (White people). A barrel-shaped man, the widest part of him was his waist. With his small head, rotund middle, and spindly legs, he looked like a cartoon character.

Although I frequented his store, we never met. I don't suppose he knew me at all. I, on the other hand, knew his schedule and all the goings-on in the parking lot. I looked forward to watching him and his lady friend in the front seat of his car. Until then, I had never seen a man and a woman entangled together in what seemed to me the most uncomfortable positions.

One day, my mother and I walked to Luckey's to buy her some underwear. We located ladies' undergarments after going down one aisle after another: we didn't know how to say "underwear" in English. From the piles of underwear, my mother picked up a pair of white nylon panties and raised them to eye level.

"I wonder if this would fit," she said.

We were alone in the aisle, protected by mounds of clothing, so I suggested she try them on. My mother glanced around, quickly slipped one foot and then the other into the panties, and pulled them up underneath her skirt.

"They fit pretty well," she said. Simultaneously, we realized taking the panties off was not going to be as easy as putting them on. A saleslady was approaching. The store suddenly had several other customers.

We froze in place. We couldn't speak the language to explain our predicament. To pantomime trying on underwear would have required my modest mother to lift up her skirt. I waited. My mother smoothed her skirt and said, "Let's go."

Outside, she squinted in the sunlight and said, "It couldn't be helped." I understood.

THREE IDENTICAL HOUSES, LIKE Monopoly game houses, sat behind Luckey's. Our house was the nearest to the parking lot. My earliest American friends lived in the other two. Joe was a Mexican boy a couple years younger, and Johnny was a Black boy of around seven. We didn't have much in common except for being children and being poor. All three of us were left on our own.

Our playground was the parking lot. We played there until dusk—until one twilight evening when the policemen came. I can't quite recall which game we were playing, but all three of us were standing around. Joe was only nine, but he was a large boy who looked at least twelve. Johnny was pudgy with big, bulging eyes that made him look perennially surprised. Then there was me, a skinny Asian girl with thick glasses and overly permed hair like the cartoon character Nancy. We were a motley trio of intermingling races that was uncommon in those times when TV shows featured mostly white Americans.

When the black-and-white police car stopped, the driver didn't bother to park between the white lines. Two officers got out of the car and swaggered toward us. One officer fingered his nightstick.

"What are you kids doing here?" he asked. Neither was smiling.

"Just playing," Joe blurted. Johnny and I were dumbstruck. The officers didn't look like they believed Joe.

"What are your names and where do you live?" the officer asked. Joe gave his name and said he lived at the yellow house. Johnny gave them his information. When my turn came, I whispered my name and pointed to my house only a yard away.

Our answers seemed to satisfy them. The officer assumed the official position—legs spread wide, arms folded. In a commanding voice, he gave us an order: "Don't let us catch you loitering around here again. You hear?" We nodded, even smart-mouthed Joe.

We had lost our play area. A little bit of our innocence was lost that dusky evening, too. From that day on, I was on the lookout for black-and-white cars. A new country. Different rules.

MY PETS

G ROWING UP IN UNRYUL, where I lived with my grandparents, the concept of "pet" was foreign. In the large
enclosed courtyard, chickens roamed freely. They were not
pets. They were potential food.

One week my mother made "chick" soup and fed it to me
for supper each day. When I asked why I was the only one
eating a chick a day, she said a chick was not enough food for a
grown person, but it was just the right portion for a little girl.
Some sickness had been spreading among the chickens. She
saved the chicks from this illness by making me chick soup.

Cats, too, hung out in the courtyard, but they were not
pets, either. They earned their keep by catching mice. My
view on animals changed when we came to the United States
and I wanted to be an American.

The year was 1952. Since we had gotten off the boat a year
before, Omai and I considered ourselves old-timers, not like the
newcomers who were commonly labeled as FOBs (Fresh Off
the Boat). That year, when I was eleven, I became a pet owner.

Since coming to America, we had not met many people.
Not including the neighbors, the handful we had gotten ac-
quainted with were all Koreans. Most of the older people were
immigrants from the 1920s and 1930s. The younger Koreans
were primarily students. They were called "foreign" students.

One student who befriended us was studying at UCLA. About twenty-five, he was gaunt and pale, with high cheekbones, and I would have described him as ascetic if I had known such a word. His physical appearance belied his exuberant personality.

I still remember him describing in detail, with great zest, how he made chicken soup. "I cook the whole chicken—everything. Enough water to completely cover it. Put the lid on and cook slowly until the flesh falls off the bone."

I stifled my laughter as he was instructing the maestro of chicken soup, my mother! Without missing a beat, he extolled the health benefits of his soup.

As a foreign student, he didn't have much money, which was not conducive to the Korean custom of bringing a gift to a host. One day when he came to visit, he brought two cardboard boxes bound with string. As soon as he saw me, he thrust the boxes at me.

"I have presents for you," he said, smiling. What could these ordinary boxes contain?

"Open them," he said. I untied the string he had knotted to secure the lid on the smaller box and found two white rats with ropy pink tails twice the length of their bodies. I was attracted to them and repulsed by them at the same time. I certainly did not want to touch them. My mother must have sensed what I felt. She came to my rescue before ungracious words could be spoken.

"Look at them! Where did they come from?" she asked.

"They are from my laboratory at school." He picked one up and stroked its back. "They make good pets." I wanted to be a grateful recipient. I smiled and asked if I should open the other box.

I heard scratching noises inside the box; something in it was alive. With apprehension, I pulled the lid up and found three little yellow chicks. They looked as surprised as I was. I shrieked. "Ddahk shek-gee! (Little chicks!) Did these come from your lab, too?"

He said they had, and wanted us to know the rats and the chicks had not been subjected to experiments. We were relieved—especially since he did research on leprosy!

As much as my benefactor said that rats make good pets, I just couldn't get past the stiff, worm-like tails. The following day, I gave them to my friend Joe. His stepmother liked the rats more than Joe did and frequently carried one cradled in the cleavage of her ample breasts.

My chicks did not enjoy such coziness. They stayed indoors in their early months, producing so much waste that our floor had to be covered with newspaper. Potty training was not possible. While baby chicks are cute—so small and fragile—they lose their attractiveness once they hit puberty. No more fluffy yellow feathers, no more soft pulsating bodies. They resemble those rubber chickens with long necks and scrawny bodies covered with pimply skin. Unaware of their ugliness, they strut around, ever so arrogantly. I banished them to the strip of dirt in the back.

When they were still juveniles, it was difficult to tell whether they were hens or roosters. I waited for them to become adults. The transition seemed like it happened overnight, especially with the roosters. Of the three, two were roosters. I found out that this was not good. Not good for the two roosters, and definitely not for the lone hen. The roosters fought constantly. The poor hen had no rest. The squawking, clawing, flying feathers made a war zone of our dirt patch of a yard.

The last time I saw my pets, the smaller rooster had been badly beaten up by the other. It had lost most of its feathers, exposing gored, bare skin, but was still sporting a torn comb.

The birds disappeared, and I did not know what had happened to them. However, the next day, the chicken soup my mother made really tasted good.

My attempt at cultural assimilation as an American pet owner was over.

LEARNING ENGLISH

IT WAS MY FIRST day of school in America. I had awakened early and washed my face. I already knew which of my two dresses I wanted to wear. I pulled on the blue plaid dress with the short, puffed sleeves and the full skirt. My mother tied the sash into a perfect bow in the back. I put on my new Buster Brown shoes. I had wanted white airy sandals with ankle straps, but my mother said that these sturdy shoes would last much longer.

I had trouble taming my hair. In preparation for school, my mother had treated me to a perm. We figured this was a splendid idea as American girls have curly hair and the stinky permanent solution would wipe out the colony of head lice I still harbored. My straight hair must have drunk the solution dry. I ended up with wire coils, hair so bushy my face was hidden from view. My mother rubbed sesame oil on it, to make it shiny and full.

Since I was now going to attend an American school, my Omai thought that I should use my baptismal name given to me by the French priest who baptized me when I was a baby. I would not be Woon-hee. My name henceforth would be Joanna.

An American neighbor girl and her younger brother came to take me to school. She was older than I was, maybe twelve, but much taller. My mother said Americans were taller than Koreans because of the plentiful food. I liked the girl and her brother and wished I could speak English.

We walked the same route as the trolley ran on Vermont Avenue, from Jefferson Boulevard to Adams Boulevard. The siblings walked a few steps ahead, talking and laughing. I followed, stopping when they stopped at the lights and lagging behind a few paces when walking. Frequently, the girl turned around to keep an eye on me. She smiled, but I was too apprehensive to return her smile.

We passed a beautiful church. I had to stop and look up to see the spires made with metal lace. We turned the corner at Adams, and there loomed a building that turned out to be our school. The brother broke off from his sister and went inside. The girl steered me to the entrance and walked me to a classroom on the first floor.

A nun stood at the door, dressed in a long black robe with a wimple framing her round face, just like the nuns I had known back in Korea. She looked jolly—plump, short, and cuddly. I could only guess, from the tone of her foreign words, that she had welcomed me to her class. All I could feel was my pounding heart. Without understanding a single word of English, I felt like I had been thrown into the Pacific when I didn't know how to swim.

I was the only new child in the class. The school year began in September and I didn't start school until December. The tiny desks were in neat rows. Some children were already sitting at their desks, and others were still arriving. I stood, waiting. The nun approached and spoke to me. The only thing that registered was the high pitch of her voice. She steered me by my shoulders and pointed to an empty desk seat in the middle of the second row. I slid my body into the chair. I lifted the desk lid and put in my lunch wrapped in my mother's handmade cloth, the size of a handkerchief.

Surrounded by small children no older than six, I felt tall and awkward. But I was thankful that I was small and skinny for my age. I was ten years old! I hadn't expected to repeat first grade. These younger children were cute. Most had sandy hair and blue eyes and freckles. I checked the teeth of those around me. They were in various stages of losing their baby teeth.

The class began. It took months before I mastered the morning ritual. The teacher was addressed as "Sister." Each morning, Sister said, "Good morning, boys and girls." The children responded with "Good morning, Sister." We stood and recited the Pledge of Allegiance. We made the sign of the cross before Sister said a prayer and crossed our hearts again at the end of the prayer.

That first day, the only activity I participated in was standing. When the children stood, I stood. That much I could follow. At my desk, I sat straight and folded my hands on my lap, the way my teacher in Korea had instructed.

I heard the Sister's shrill voice, but I was clueless. I might as well have been deaf. My sight was the only sense working. When Sister talked, I looked at her. When the children talked, I looked at them. When they stood, I stood. When they sat, I sat. I watched everything . . . except I wasn't observant enough on one important detail of classroom deportment.

I followed Sister's movements with my eyes as she came toward me. I was eye level with the rosary around her waist. She spoke. I looked up at her. Getting no response from me, she pushed her long sleeves up to her elbows and turned her hands with palms facing up. Still, I sat there. She lowered her hands and grabbed each of my hands in turn and positioned them before me, palms face up. I held that position. Satisfied, she dug deep inside a fold in her skirt and brought forth a twelve-inch wooden ruler. Before I could blink, she slapped the ruler down on my open palms. Crack! It was like being struck by lightning.

I was dumbfounded. I sat in the same position with my stinging palms extended, paralyzed with fear and confusion. The Sister broke the silence with her English words. Other students understood, but getting hit with the ruler did not help me comprehend her words.

I lowered my gaze. In Korea, a sign of disrespect is to look an adult in the eye, especially when one has done something wrong. From the corner of my eye, I saw Sister's hand reaching for mine. Talking continuously, she took my hands and firmly placed them on top of my desk. I glanced at her quickly. She didn't appear to be mad. Around the room, all of the children sat up straight with their hands folded on top of their desks. I took the cue. My hands were glued to the top of my desk for the rest of the day.

In America, hands stay on top of the desk, not hidden under the desk, just the opposite of what I had learned in Korea.

The rest of the morning passed slowly. Sister talked. The children talked and sang. I sat. At last, lunchtime came. I followed my classmates out to the patio. They climbed onto the bench seats attached to long tables. I sat down hesitantly. I needn't have been so cautious. The little girl who sat next to me started talking to me as if I were an old friend.

She talked and talked. It didn't seem to matter to her that I was not replying. Other children joined in. I was grateful that these little ones treated me as one of them. Some had metal lunch boxes with pictures painted on the lids. Others had brown paper bags. I untied the cloth wrap revealing a bar of Hershey's milk chocolate. My lunch mates went quiet. They wanted some chocolate. I broke off a square and offered it to the girl next to me. She was delighted, and gave me half of her bologna sandwich in return. I didn't know what the sandwich was called: all I knew was that I was eating an American food.

The evening before, my mother had asked, "Shall I make a bento box for you?"

"I don't know. What do American children eat?" I asked, but I knew she didn't know the answer either. I had worried that taking our small tin container filled with rice and one pan-chan (side dish) might make me too conspicuous. It was bad enough that I could speak only Korean, but to show up with rice and chopsticks would make me feel even more different. We decided I would take the only American food we knew.

That was a wonderful stroke of luck as, with each square of candy I passed out, I became an instant friend to my classmates. After school that day, I described to my mother what American children ate. For the first time, I was telling her how to prepare food. Much later, I taught her an American word pronounced "sandaweechi."

Several days later, two new students joined our class. I was elated. They didn't speak English either! The little girl with brown curly hair, much younger than I, came from France. She could have been an American girl—no one would have known the difference if she didn't speak. I didn't catch her name but everybody knew the name of the new boy, even I did.

Sister couldn't help herself calling his name in her high, singsong voice, "Hey soos." I didn't know "Hey soos" was the pronunciation of Jesus in his native country. Jesus was taller than I, but after a while, I deduced he was much younger.

The three of us non-English speakers were attracted to each other—or maybe the Sister sat us together. We sat together, deaf and dumb in the ways of the English language. The French girl spoke French, Jesus spoke Spanish, and I spoke Korean. Having no common language, we pantomimed.

Jesus was the icebreaker. He spat out a lump of saliva on his palm and mashed it dry with his other palm. We watched him grinding his palms together. When satisfied that he had done a thorough job of this, he licked his palm that held the dried saliva. We watched as if he were performing a magic trick. Then he sniffed it. He crinkled his nose and made a wrinkled face. We waited. He thrust his palm for us to smell. Curious, we both dove our faces to his extended hand. I took a big sniff. The odor was putrid, like the smell on my finger when I dug into my belly button.

The French girl and I replicated his trick. Somehow, our odor wasn't as potent as his. The three of us engaged in this process without exchanging a word in any language. How were we to learn English when our main communication mode was spitting and smelling?

There were no English as a Second Language (ESL) programs. One learned in a "sink or swim" mode, a strategy known today as a "total immersion program." I sat in the first grade for four months with no apparent progress in learning English. In retrospect, it was my incubation period. The first graders, as it turned out, were the best possible teachers for me to learn the language. Their sentences were simple. They repeated the same words over and over. They talked constantly. Most importantly, they accepted me as one of them. I felt comfortable trying out my "baby steps" using English with them, knowing they wouldn't make fun of me.

Our class learned the alphabet by singing the letters to the tune of "Twinkle, Twinkle, Little Star." Later, the students struggled to decipher words written on the big poster book in front of the class. The stories featured Dick, Jane, Sally, and Spot, the family's dog. I learned to speak and read English at the same time.

I still have my first dictionary: *A Picture Dictionary for Boys and Girls* by Alice Scott, M.A. It contains more than 3,600 words and over 1,700 pictures in color. The front cover depicts a boy and a girl, both cherub-faced with the features I considered so American: light brown hair, round eyes, and protruding noses. I studied the words in my dictionary every night. To study meant looking at the word and the picture for that word. I couldn't pronounce the words yet, since I didn't know how the English should sound just by looking at the letters or the pictures. All I could do was look at the images, think of the words in Korean, and try to remember the string of English letters associated with each picture. I promised myself: someday I will know all these words.

I learned faster than I planned. I needed words to express an outrage when a neighborhood friend tried to cheat in a game of jump rope. Just as I had jumped rope with my friend, Myung Ja, back in the old country, I jumped rope with a neighbor girl. She didn't look like other American girls. Yet, she didn't exactly look like a Hook-In (Black person) either. She had wiry light brown hair, a broad nose, and thick lips, but her skin was honey-colored, not dark like a Hook-In's. She lived with her grandmother, who shared the same features.

After school, she and her grandmother would knock on my door to invite me to play. We played two games: hopscotch and jump rope. On this particular day, we happened to get two more neighborhood girls to jump rope. We tied our ropes together to make a longer one and took turns swinging the rope and jumping.

Everyone was having fun, until my neighbor friend cheated. She stepped on the rope and should have been eliminated, but she continued to skip. The girl had said something to others who were turning the rope, but I didn't hear what she said. They continued to chant a rhyme with each turn of the rope. It was my turn to go in.

The girl cheated and nothing happened. I didn't know I had so many English words stored in me. They tumbled out of my mouth, loudly, angrily, rapidly. Who knows if they made any sense. Just to make sure she understood, I grabbed my rope, untied it from hers, and strode back to my house.

I have been speaking English ever since.

MATH WHIZ

I BECAME A CELEBRITY at my new elementary school—an unlikely celebrity! Sister Marilyn, my first-grade teacher, the very same nun who hit my hands with a ruler on my first day, was my promoter. Things changed between the Sister and me.

While I worked to catch up with my classmates in English, I found myself far ahead of them in mathematics. The first graders were still learning to recognize Arabic numerals. I had learned my numbers four years earlier when I was in first grade in Korea. Sister Marilyn must have known this. She gave me a worksheet with arithmetic problems. I relished the chance to do familiar work at which I excelled. I solved the problems quickly. I laid down my pencil and folded my hands on top of my desk.

Sister Marilyn picked up the sheet and looked it over. She smiled. I sat up taller, feeling as though I had grown a few inches.

The next day, she called my name, crooked her fingers toward herself, and said, "Come." I was hesitant, since the signal for "come" in Korea is a wave of one's hand, the same gesture I found out later indicated "goodbye" in America. Standing by the door, she kept nodding her head and motioning her cupped hand. When I went to her, she took my hand and led me to the staircase. We walked up to the second floor.

The classroom door on which she knocked had a big sign with a number four on it. She opened the door and led me inside. All the boys and girls turned around to look at us. The Sister must have introduced me: I recognized two words she spoke, "Joanna" and "Korea."

She led me to the front of the class. Now, I stood facing the children—forty American children with eighty eyes—looking at me, a small Korean girl.

Sister Marilyn said something to the other nun, the teacher of this fourth-grade class. The teacher wrote with a chalk on the left side of the blackboard an addition problem: four addends of three digits. She wrote the same problem on the right side. She called on one of her students to come up to the board. Sister Marilyn placed me in front of the problem on the right, and the boy stood facing the problem on the left. She dispensed a piece of chalk to each of us, then said, "Go." The boy began calculating. I figured that I was to solve the problem also.

I did the calculation in Korean as fast as I could and wrote the answer. The boy was still computing. Sister Marilyn beamed. For three more rounds I was matched with three different students. Each time, I beat them in accuracy and time.

The following day, Sister Marilyn knocked on the door of a fifth-grade class. The fifth graders were working on multiplication and division problems. I had mastered my multiplication tables up to nine during the war with the help of the teacher who had lived in the churchyard. She taught a short-cut method to memorizing the tables, a method so fixed in my mind that to this day I can only multiply in Korean. That morning, I solved problem after problem in the fifth-grade class. Once again, I performed exceedingly well for my teacher.

In Korea, I would have been assigned to the fifth grade, but the war interrupted my schooling after the third grade. I hoped that this fifth-grade class was the last one we would visit, but Sister Marilyn had other ideas.

The next week, we climbed another set of stairs to a sixth-grade class. The students were large. Their desks were big. Once again, I was matched with American students, one after another. The arithmetic problems got increasingly difficult: five-digit multiplicands by three-digit multipliers. Same level of difficulty for the division problems. One problem took the entire board space to solve. I saved time by calculating mentally.

I must have appeared like a genius—the only Asian girl in the entire school, who didn't seem to talk but traveled to different classes solving arithmetic problems with accuracy and speed. I had no awareness of how I came across to my fellow students. All I wanted was to do well so that Sister Marilyn would be pleased. Like a monkey performing tricks for its master, I was Sister Marilyn's prize pet. On the way back to our classroom, she'd whistle a little tune, and we'd skip so that the beads around her waist would jingle. Sister Marilyn took good care of me that first year of school.

Looking back at young me attending a new school in a foreign country, I see how much I wanted to be an American girl. In Korea, I couldn't wait to go to school. School was so much fun: learning to read, write, count, sing, paint, and play games. Even during the winter vacations, the first thing I did each morning was my homework. One of my favorite assignments was to go outdoors after snowfall and look for animal paw prints in the snow. We were to draw these prints and identify the animal on the handout booklet. At the American school, I hadn't known what to expect. If I had been given a choice about going to classroom after classroom solving math problems, would young me have said "No" to Sister Marilyn? I doubt it. It turned out that being a math whiz led me to be more confident in a new environment. On my way to becoming an American girl: from getting my hand slapped with a ruler to becoming the teacher's pet.

MY MOTHER'S SHOES

Los Angeles, 1952

I WAS A LATCHKEY child before the term was even invented. My house key hung on a long piece of thick twine cut from my mother's laundry line. Each morning, I put it on like a necklace. I would have felt incomplete without it. My mother was a single mom before that term too was coined. She was a working mom when most mothers were homemakers. Immigrant life was makeshift. In retrospect, we were ahead of our time, despite how backward we may have seemed in the eyes of our American neighbors.

In the mornings, my mother crept out of our bed when it was still dark. I'd roll over to the middle of the bed and curl up in a fetal position and sleep until she came to wake me before she left for work. I knew I had gotten one and a half more hours of sleep while she prepared breakfast for me. She made our traditional Korean breakfast of rice and soup. On the kitchen table, she set a rice bowl and a soup bowl, both covered with lids to keep the food warm. She also set down a brown lunch bag. I knew the contents: a bologna sandwich and an orange. My American lunch, every day.

GETTING HERSELF READY FOR work didn't take long. Omai had one suit she wore to church on Sunday, two dresses, and one sweater that we had found in the donation bin among the clothes that were intended to be shipped to Korea. She had two pairs of shoes—men's work boots, also retrieved from the donation box, and her all-purpose, everyday shoes. She carried her boots to wear at work. They were old and tired—scuffed, dirty, the tongues all dried out, heels so worn on the outer edges that when she stood, she was perpetually bow-legged. She couldn't walk in them. She lugged those boots, clump, clump, so that her small feet wouldn't fall out of them.

Her everyday shoes were white pumps. One day, I had a bright idea. I painted blue shoe polish on her pumps. I said, "Now, people will think you have another pair of shoes." She didn't protest nor scold me. She was just too tired to be bothered with the color of her shoes.

My mother, who never had a formal job back in Korea, worked a variety of menial jobs that required no English. She complained most about the assembly line work at the canning factory. Even my mother could pronounce its name: Jan-U-Wine. Over the years that she worked there, I became familiar with a big cast of characters through my mother's eyes. The most repugnant person was Pablo, the foreman. My introduction to Pablo began shortly after she started working, at dinnertime.

"Pa-bu-lo is myuk-ja-goo," she said.

"What do you mean he is a frog?" I asked.

"Mrs. Yim told me that Pabulo comes from Myukjagoo." My mother's Korean ears translated foreign words to words that sound similar in Korean. So the word "Mexico" became Myuk-jagoo. She thought she was pronouncing an English word.

I hated Pabulo for making my mother's life miserable. Every evening, my mother unloaded to me about her day at work. Pablo was a ladies' man and he had a "harem" at the factory. I thought it strange that all the workers at the factory were from other countries. Where did the Americans work? There were women from Germany, Japan, Mexico, and two from Korea.

"Pabulo is a bad man," my mother said as she set the soup bowls on our kitchen table.

She spat out the words nah bboon nom (bad man). "He came right behind the German woman and grabbed her jut (breast) and started massaging with his grubby hands. And the woman let him."

My mother sat down to eat her dinner. She was just warming up. All she swallowed during the day came spewing out. "Later, on my way back from my break, I saw them kissing. Yes, he is a yahman (savage), for sure." She paused to take a sip of water. "If you let Pabulo touch you, like the German woman, then he lets you work longer. Other people like me, he says, 'Go home.' The first time he told me 'go home,' I didn't know what that meant. I asked Mrs. Yim and she translated. Now, when he comes around, I know. That's the worst thing, to be sent home. But that man also plays favorites in other ways. The women who let him touch them, they get easier jobs like sweeping the floor. For me, I always get stuck with packing 'supahnishi-rice.'"

Omai described the packing process, how she and others stood by a long table on which a conveyor belt with cans streamed by. From above where they stood, hot gobs of reddish "supahnishi" rice dropped down in front of them. Their job was to scoop up the rice and pack it into the cans as they moved along on the conveyor belt. "I get so hot from the steam of hot rice, my eyes sting from all the sweat. I have to keep shoving the rice into cans. There's no chance to wipe my face. Lots of my sweat dropped in those cans along with the rice."

Sometimes, I wanted her to stop talking. I lived her anguish as if I were there at the factory. I did not want my mother to go to work. How I wished I could go to work in her place.

She learned more English at the factory. Besides "go home," Pablo inadvertently taught my mother another word. Since I had started school, I was my mother's source for anything pertaining to the English language and American ways. During dinner one evening, she asked, "What does 'sahru-mada-becchu' mean? The words sounded like 'sahru-mada' and 'becchu' put together."

I knew what sahru-mada meant. Since the Japanese had occupied Korea for thirty-five years, many Koreans spoke Japanese. "Sahru-mada" meant underwear in Japanese, I had been told. "Becchu" is a Korean word for cabbage. I tried to put the two words' meanings together. Underwear-cabbage. It couldn't be a literal translation. Maybe Omai was trying to find familiar words within unfamiliar English phrases as she often did.

I asked, "Who said that and under what circumstances?"

She said that Pablo always said it in an angry tone. I repeated sahru-mada-becchu over and over, faster and faster, until it sounded like an English expression I had heard but knew not to use in polite company: son of a bitch.

After we finished eating and the dishes were washed, my mother filled a small round pan with warm water to soak her feet. Her small feet had angry-looking toes. The underside of her toes looked like the diseased flesh of dead fish—white crust with pinkish flesh where the skin had split. Even after a good soaking, the smell of her feet was worse than the sight. It became a game for us. I would dry her feet and take a whiff. Then I would shout, "They smell!" I rolled onto my back as if the putrid potency had knocked me down. Oddly, I became addicted to that smell.

Home by myself after school, I often waited until it was time to walk to the bus stop on the main street to meet Omai at the end of her workday. Sometimes, I got there early to read the comic books displayed at the front of the nearby big market. No one seemed to mind that I stood there reading Archie comic books while waiting for my mother's bus. Veronica and Betty, the two girls in the comics, became my imaginary friends, especially Betty. I wanted to dress like her. When I saw my mother's bus approaching, I replaced the comic book on the stand and waited for the bus to stop. The two of us walked the three blocks to our rented house.

One day, the afternoon drizzle turned into a torrential rainstorm and I did not walk to the bus stop but waited for her at home, watching out the parlor window. Time ticked by slowly. Streams of rain slithered down the window. I pressed my face against the pane for a sharper look. The window fogged from my breath, and I wiped it with my fist. I saw a bent figure trudging wearily on the narrow path to our house.

I opened the door. Omai's head was covered by a drenched scarf, and wisps of wet stray hair clung to her face. Her rain-soaked sweater smelled musty. Water dripped onto her feet. The shoes I had so meticulously painted blue had turned into a mottled mess, with blue streaks bleeding into the white. I wanted to cry, but tears could not wash away the image of my mother in those shoes.

CLIFTON'S CAFETERIA

S OME OF MY HAPPIEST memories from those early years in California were the visits from Little Brother. He attended college in San Francisco, and I looked forward to his visits during school breaks.

He treated me to lunch at Clifton's, which I remember as a magical place with fake tall trees, waterfalls, and lifelike animals. As soon as you entered the restaurant, you left the bustle of downtown Los Angeles. Inside, the waterfall cascaded to a pond. The falling water's tinkling sound seemed to be a rhythmic accompaniment to the beautiful music floating in the air. I would hum "The Blue Danube" long after a visit, although at the time, I did not know the title of this waltz.

In the dim lighting, with the many varieties of plants and giant faux redwoods and life-size taxidermy that included animated raccoons and a bear holding a fishing pole, I felt like I was in a deep forest.

I liked the cafeteria style of dining. I didn't know the word "cafeteria" nor did I know the English words for the food items either. Some foods I didn't even recognize. There were so many choices, and all I had to do was point. Jell-O, for example. I liked its softness and sweetness and how it jiggled in my mouth.

After Clifton's, we walked down Broadway to the movies. Children got in free, back in the 1950s. I was thankful for that, as I didn't understand complex English, and it would have been a shame to pay when I could not understand most of the dialogue.

I loved the musicals and seeing the beautiful women and handsome men in Technicolor. My brother bought bonbons. I enjoyed the cold smooth chocolate when I popped one in my mouth and savored the soft ice cream after the chocolate melted. From time to time, my brother would lean over and whisper a brief synopsis of what was happening on the screen. From watching and his updates, I pretty much figured out the story. I always liked the ending when the couple kissed, and then, accompanied by the swelling music, in large letters, "The End." I could read those words.

WEDNESDAY NIGHT
WRESTLING

Los Angeles, 1953

THE THIRD WEDNESDAY EVENING of every month was my special night with Omai. No matter how tired my mother was from her "standing only" job at Jan-U-Wine, on this night, I could tell from the sound of her footsteps coming up the narrow cement path to our house how much she always looked forward to this evening.

We had now been in America for two years. We had settled into our "upgraded" rental, a small house in the back of a larger one on 31st Street, a half block from busy Vermont Avenue. This house even had a front porch equipped with a swinging chair. On the third Wednesdays, swaying on the swing, I waited for Omai. A part of settled life entailed routines—a sense of planting roots in the new country. And did we ever!

We discovered wrestling. Many years later, when I fancied myself a sophisticated lady, my new women friends asked what sports I liked. Many of them played tennis and golf. I was versed in calling the tennis instrument a racquet, but I made a blunder referring to the golf clubs as sticks. The cordial ladies then asked what spectator sports I liked. Little did I realize that my passion for wrestling was not one cultured ladies shared. "Oh, really?" one said as she glanced at the others.

Back in the golden years of wrestling—how my mother and I enjoyed it! We knew all the wrestlers of that era: "Nature Boy" Buddy Rogers, with the platinum blond wavy locks; Bobo Brazil, with a mahogany-shaded muscular physique like a living statue; Sandor Szabo, one of the good guys; the flamboyant Gorgeous George, with long golden tresses and flowing silk and chiffon robes; Mr. Moto, an enhanced caricature of a Japanese sumo wrestler, with his exotic pre-fight ritual of squats and sprinkling of salt to the four corners of the ring; Fred Blassie, who was as famous as Buddy Rogers; and my favorite, Ray "Thunder" Stern—the crush of my prepubescent girlhood. Compared to other wrestlers, he was short with a compact body. He was also only nineteen. Ray "Thunder" Stern fought fairly. He was one of the good guys. Whenever he wrestled, I was paralyzed with fear that he would get hurt. Besides my chant for him to kill his opponent, I silently prayed to God to help him do just that.

One Wednesday night, I got lucky. At the Olympic Auditorium, we queued up and bought our tickets to sit in the back of the auditorium, far from the ring. Usually, all the expensive seats were occupied, but that night I spotted an empty seat in the third row from the ring. I kept my eye on that seat for a couple of rounds. Then I tapped my mother's shoulder and said, "Look over there, Omai. Do you see the empty seat toward the front?" She sat upright and peered where I pointed. "Can I go down to the seat?" I asked.

"You can go. I can see you from here," she said.

Before the next event, a tag team, I made my way to the front. I was nervous and prepared myself to turn back if anybody objected to my intrusion. I took "my" seat between men who minded their own business. I don't think they even noticed me, since they were so wrapped up with what went on in the ring.

The audience became frenzied. We stamped our feet. A volcanic eruption wouldn't have been as thunderous as when the crowd got up and started jumping up and down in rhythm, fists thrust upward, in sync with the chorus of "Kill him! Kill him!" Usually, I had to stand on my chair to see the action, but not that night.

I was so close that the wrestlers' sweat sprayed me. That close. In a tag team event, two wrestlers on one team take turns wrestling the other team. The script was always the same: Good versus bad. The crowd cheered the "good" wrestler as he worked the leg of his opponent, grinding it back to the torso. Someone shouted, "Break his leg!" The bad guy grappled for his opponent's hair, but our hero was relentless and kept on grinding the bad guy's leg. All of a sudden, the bad guy's partner rushed into the ring, delivered a big hammer blow across the back of the good guy, picked him up like a slab of meat, hoisting him on his shoulder, and spun "airplanes." All the while he was moving toward the rope—on my side. I knew what came next in this story. That bad guy was going to throw the good guy out of the ring. It looked like he might land right on my lap—all three hundred pounds of him. I jumped up and took a leap back two rows and made a flawless landing: A man caught me. I didn't want to be smashed under the wrestler. And he did land right in the seat that I—all eighty pounds of me—had just abandoned!

At the time, my mother and I did not know that wrestling had a reputation of being pseudo-athletic entertainment. We did not know that the fights were staged, not real. With all the sweat, blood, head-body slams, piledrivers, dropkicks, high flying, biting, gouging of eyes, how could it be fake?

What we enjoyed about wrestling, I think now, was that it was our version of a morality play where the theme was good versus evil. The wrestlers were portrayed as heroes and villains. The audience—like a Greek chorus—cheered for the hero and booed at the villain, one collective psyche. We were a polyglot group of men, women, and children of varying ethnicities and cultures. The high drama everyone shared helped us understand one another's languages. The Koreans, including Omai and me, shouted "Ju-gi-rah." The Mexicans, "Matalo." We all issued the same directive, and my mother and I learned to chant it in English: "Kill him! Kill him!"

The third Wednesday night at the Olympic Auditorium was a respite from the daily grind of immigrant life. There, while the morality tales played out, life seemed simple and pure. For my mother, it was a break from the daily toil at the Jan-U-Wine factory. Every day, she got up at dawn, made my breakfast and lunch, and rode the bus to the factory.

Years later, I found a black-and-white photo of her standing by a conveyor belt. She wore a hairnet with a white crown like a nurse's cap and a long rubber apron, the kind one pulls over the head and ties in the back. She stood stuffing Spanish rice into nineteen-ounce metal cans transported on the interminable conveyor belt. Eight hours of standing and stuffing ever-moving cans, grateful to bring home $8.00 at the end of her shift. She deserved more than a monthly night out of entertainment.

Many years later, we happened to see a wrestling match on TV. We smiled, thinking back to our wrestling days. As we watched, she asked, "Juh-guh, jong mal i-ni? (Is it real?)"

I thought for a moment as to how I should respond.

"Wrestling was real back then," I replied. The Korean word, jong mal, means true. It was true for us.

HIGH SCHOOL YEARS

Los Angeles, 1955

M Y MOTHER KNEW NOTHING about my grade placement at school. She knew only what I told her. We trusted that the Sisters' decisions were the best for an immigrant child.

I had been in America for four years when I entered high school. After my first year in the first grade at the age of ten, the following year, I skipped to third grade and then to fourth grade the next year. After two and a half years of schooling, my English must have been good enough: I skipped grades five and six and advanced to grade seven when I was thirteen years old.

At fourteen, I was finally promoted to ninth grade. Skipping these grades was not due to my intellectual brilliance. It had to do with age-appropriate placement. In order to be placed in a certain grade, the student must meet the age eligibility requirement.

High school was a totally different experience from grade school. Instead of learning in a self-contained class with one teacher, I attended many classes, each with a different teacher. There were many more students and I did not know any of them from the year before, since I had skipped the eighth grade.

I missed my old classmates, even though they were younger, and I worried about fitting in with my new peers. I had not minded wearing the same dress day in and day out when I was in grade school, but now I felt self-conscious. I attended a Catholic school, but we did not wear uniforms. I wished we did. To this day, I am an advocate for uniforms. They equalize the rich and poor, at least in appearance. The only Asian girl at this high school, I wanted more than anything to be like American girls. Although Omai made me a full gathered rayon skirt, I wanted a poodle skirt like the other girls wore.

Fred—a student who had come from Germany—instigated an incident that mortified me. He was a tall boy with apple cheeks, who hung around with several other students from Germany and Austria. These students became proficient in English far faster than I, it seemed. Maybe it had to do with their intelligence, or it might have been because the German alphabet is the same as the English alphabet. They spoke German to each other, and I envied the camaraderie among them. One day, Fred started laughing as soon as I entered our Physics classroom. He pointed at me, while clutching his stomach with his other hand. Finally, he composed himself and addressed me in a loud voice: "I saw you in physical education. Where did you get those pants?" He burst into laughter again.

I felt my face grow hot. I had worn the plaid pants that my mother and I had retrieved a number of years ago from the donation bin when we lived in the back storage shed. They now fit me—but they didn't help me to fit in. I was so relieved when several months later, we girls got gym uniforms—purple bloomers and matching colored tops. I looked ridiculous with my skinny legs sticking out of my puffed-out bloomers, but I didn't care. At least I fit in, in gym class.

I had one dress that I wore most days. My mother made it, as it was much cheaper for her to sew than to purchase one. When we went to Woolworth's to buy the fabric, I was quite taken with a pink cotton cloth imprinted with tiny Japanese wooden dolls. The dolls were as thin as a pencil and about half an inch in height, with a small circle for a head. That fabric would be perfect for a shirtwaist dress of the kind in fashion.

I wore the dress so often, other students thought pink was my favorite color and nicknamed me "Pinky." I liked that my small group of friends cared enough to give me a nickname, though little did they know that it was my only dress.

I did not mind having so few outfits, when I thought about it. I saw how hard my mother was working so that I could get an education. For a woman born to gentry, life in America, a life of displacement, was alien to her. I did not like her working so hard at the menial jobs she held, and I wished I could grow up fast so I could relieve her from her drudgery.

She now rose at 3:00 a.m. to get to her factory job, making artificial flowers. She never complained; she had a higher purpose. She validated her commitment to me often saying: "Education is important." I do not have a wide vocabulary in Korean but the word joong-hyo—important—was indelibly imprinted in my mind. From a young age, she instilled these words in me: education is important.

My mother's drive to better my life's chances knew no boundaries. She asked her Korean friends if they knew of another job. Whenever she heard of a lead, she went in search of that job. Even though she couldn't speak English, my mother managed to communicate with sheer gumption and charm. She had what the Koreans call "noon-chi," the ability to assess a situation with her eyes (noon), with a heightened sense of perception (chi).

One day, when she came home from her cleaning job at the piano store, she asked, "How would you like to learn to play the piano?"

I was taken aback. "Muyah? (What?)"

"There's a piano I can buy very cheap. The manager said I can pay a small amount each payday. Girls from good families all know how to play the piano."

The piano she bought on a payment plan was an upright. Made of particleboard, the exterior was covered in beige and brown vinyl. Embossed on the vinyl, a pattern of tiny cowboys twirled lassos. It was one of a kind. I have never seen a piano like it since.

What good was a piano if I didn't know how to play? My mother had it all figured out—the way to pay for my piano lessons. She asked Mr. Choy if he would be interested in having dinner each day. Mr. Choy was a sixty-five-year-old single man, small in stature, and mild mannered. He always wore a suit and a fedora. According to the story from my mother's friend, he had a wife in North Korea when he left to study in America. He had been in his early twenties then. Once Korea was divided into two countries, he couldn't return to the North, and he never saw his wife again. Mr. Choy was the editor of the Korean newspaper in Los Angeles and well-known in the Korean community.

When I heard this story, I felt sorry for Mr. Choy, living a lonely life without his wife all those years, and I decided to be especially nice to him, now that he would be joining us for dinner each night. I could set the clock by his punctuality. He arrived to our house promptly at 6:30 p.m. After the greetings were out of the way, he sat in our parlor and watched the evening news while my mother was busily preparing the supper.

At first, I didn't like him changing the television channel to the news station, since I found the news boring. And besides, I thought he shouldn't be watching our television. It had taken us a long time to buy a secondhand set and we watched it only on Sunday night when our favorite shows aired, *I Love Lucy* and *The Ed Sullivan Show*. We limited our use so the TV wouldn't break down. My mother even made a cover for it. But after I heard about Mr. Choy's sad life, I turned the television set to *The Huntley-Brinkley Report* on NBC as soon as I saw him at the door.

Mr. Choy became a part of our family as the years went by. The arrangement was mutually beneficial. He was alone and did not cook, and he enjoyed my mother's cooking as well as her company. My mother had become an expert at stretching her money for meals. With the same allotment she set aside for groceries each week, she was able to feed one more. The money from Mr. Choy paid for my weekly piano lessons.

I gained another advantage by playing the piano. My mother forbade me to wash the dishes! My hands were "piano hands," she said. I took full advantage of her decision. While she did the dishes, I played the piano fortissimo to show her my gratitude.

Sister Noel was our school's music teacher and my piano teacher. I went to the convent for my lessons. One day, Sister Noel asked if I would like to play the harp. The instrument sat in an alcove, so magnificent with the gilded, curvaceous frame lined with strings from top to bottom, so exquisite I wondered how anyone could touch it.

In answer, I could only nod. That evening, I told my mother I would be taking up the harp. I didn't know then and I still don't know now what the Korean word is for harp, so I just said the English word.

"What is ha-ah-pu?" Omai asked. I showed her my new music book. On the cover was a drawing of a harp. She had never seen this instrument.

In my enthusiasm to learn to play it, I didn't think of the financial aspects of adding harp lessons on top of the piano lessons. Most likely, Sister Noel charged nominally, but when we were barely making ends meet, music lessons were luxuries. My mother never burdened me about money. Soon after the commencement of my harp lessons, my mother's evenings were taken up with piecework. There is no Korean equivalent word for "piecework." Even my mother said "peesu wohku," as if these were Korean words.

Her friends were old-time Koreans, much older than my mother, who had turned fifty years of age in 1955. These older women were picture brides of Korean men who came to America in the 1920s and 1930s. When my mother told me this, I wasn't sure what she was talking about.

She explained that the early emigrants from Korea to America were men. When they had saved enough money to purchase a bride, they sent their money and their photographs to a matchmaker in the old country. The matchmaker worked with prospective brides and their families to select a suitable match. Then the matchmaker sent the pictures of the prospective brides. The man picked his future mate from among the photos and the match became official with a legal contract.

Coming from a higher-class status (Yangban) was important to my mother. The early immigrants to America were predominantly peasants searching for a better future. The women who became picture brides were equally lower-class. My mother said, "No Yangban family would consent to send their daughter as a sajin sinbu (picture bride)."

My mother relayed what these women told her of their lives. Sometimes when they arrived in America they discovered that the man they'd seen in the photo was not the man who showed up at the port. I said to my mother, "No wonder Mrs. Lim is twice the size of Mr. Lim!" If she wanted to, Mrs. Lim could pick up her husband with just one hand. I wondered how these picture brides could fall in love with their husbands when they only saw photographs of them. They were brave to cross the Pacific Ocean to marry strangers.

Having been in this country for many decades, the picture brides were Americanized. They often sprinkled in English words when speaking in Korean. Most had adopted American first names such as Sarah or Mabel. Some of them even looked like American ladies! For example, Mrs. Park wore the latest styles with matching shoes and purse and her hair coiffed in a poodle hairstyle. Most importantly, they were the informal resource center for jobs for the newly arrived immigrants. They served as go-betweens for workers such as my mother and clients who were looking for people to do piecework.

The first piecework my mother took in was making little boxes for jewelry. Mrs. Park brought a large carton to our house. In it were the cardboard sides, bottoms, and lids, and white satin squares of the unassembled boxes. She demonstrated how to assemble the box and fold the satin piece before gluing it to line the box.

Each evening, after my mother washed the dishes, she'd spread out all these paper products and methodically and quickly assemble them into boxes. She'd then stack them in a neat pile. The second phase was to fold each satin square into pleats and glue it to the bottom of the box. After a while my mother's work was so perfect no one would have guessed the boxes were handmade.

When I headed to our bedroom each night, she was bent over at the kitchen table, working on the miniature boxes. I did not know when she crawled into our shared bed. I only knew that the next morning, she had filled two large cardboard cartons with her piecework.

To this day, I save every jewelry box. I think of my mother laboring over boxes like these, thinking that someone's mother made this box, even if it wasn't my mother. It takes time to assemble one of these boxes and less than sixty seconds to dismantle it.

Mrs. Park, the middleman of the piecework venture, must have been impressed with my mother's work, because my mother soon graduated to more complicated work. She made clip-on bow ties. She was pleased to reach the next level, as it meant she would make more money.

I went to the convent after school and practiced playing the harp every day for well over an hour. When the house Sister who ran the convent wanted me to conclude my practice, she paced back and forth in the foyer nearby. The nuns had to adhere to their schedules and I sometimes overstayed my time.

I practiced so much that my fingers blistered. I tried playing with Band-Aids covering the blisters, but that didn't work. In order to give my fingers a rest, I'd pretend to pluck the strings without actually touching them, so strong was my desire to practice.

When Sister Noel determined I was proficient enough to play for an audience, she registered me to play at the annual Irish Feish (Festival). I knew a little bit about the Irish. In school, there were many students with Irish surnames, like Sullivan, Flanagan, and O'Hara. St. Patrick's Day was a big occasion. Many priests were Irish.

For my debut performance at the Irish Feish, my mother made me a green skirt of shiny rayon. I felt like an Irish lass with my white blouse and green gathered skirt. The Master of Ceremonies introduced me. I wished I could have been an O'Choi, like a real Irish lass. Alas, I was the only Asian girl.

I curtsied to the audience and sat down to play. I did everything Sister Noel had taught me to do: I adjusted my seat so I could reach the pedals, checked the pedals, took a breath, and pulled the harp to my right shoulder.

My opening number was "Danny Boy." This song is a universal favorite. Even my mother knew this song. The Catholics as well as other foreigners who had come to Korea taught us the song. "Danny Boy" was beloved by all.

The audience started singing.

Oh, Danny boy, the pipes, the pipes are calling,
From glen to glen and down the mountainside,
The summer's gone and all the roses falling,
'Tis you, 'tis you must go and I must bide.

For the next part, I increased the volume to fortissimo and played glissando.

But come ye back when summer's in the meadow,
Or when the valley's hushed and white with snow.

Then I softened to pianissimo and slowed down for the ending.

'Tis I'll be here in sunshine or in shadow,
Oh Danny boy, oh Danny boy, I love you so.

The elongated "I love you so" evaporated into the air. I muffled the strings. The audience clapped and cheered. I took a bow.

They wanted me to play again.

I played "'Tis the Last Rose of Summer" next. This time no one sang along. I played it slowly. The repetitive beat with a 3/16 note followed by 1/16 note set a nostalgic mood. When the last chord evaporated into air and I stood, the audience gave me a standing ovation.

'Tis the last rose of summer, left blooming alone;
All her lovely companions are faded and gone;
No flower of her kindred, no rosebud is nigh,
To reflect back her blushes, or give sigh for sigh!

I locked gazes with Sister Noel. She smiled and clapped her hands without sound.

I wish I could have played "Danny Boy" for my mother, but she did not have the means to come to my recitals. She had to work. Every year, I attended the Irish Feish, and I still have all the medals I won at those wonderful Irish festivals.

My mother knew that I played well enough to receive all those prizes, but she never got to see her daughter perform. Her face lit up when I handed my gold medals with green ribbons to her. She purred her pleasure like a cat. I wanted her to know how much I appreciated her, and the only way I could do that was by studying hard and doing well.

When I turned sixteen, I was finally able to help my mother. I got a job at the corner Thrifty Drug Store. From our house, it took me just five minutes to walk to work.

Mr. L., the manager who hired me, was a tall man with a tinge of gray in his hair and a big, long nose. His eyes constantly roamed the store. He never smiled. He looked fierce. I was scared of him and I obeyed him.

On my first day of work, Mr. L. assigned me to the liquor department that also sold tobacco. That department was the first counter one saw upon entering the store. I stood on a platform behind the counter, and the customers had to look up to speak to me. I knew nothing about the department's inventory.

The first customer who came in that day was dressed in an ill-fitting, soiled shirt and faded pants. The stubble on his face made him look like a hobo I had seen in a comic book. At sixteen, when it came to judging age, I had two categories—young (like me) and old (like my mother). He was old. He asked for "Boone's Farm Apple something."

I said, "Excuse me?"

"It's the name of a wine," he said. "You have to go in there to get it." He pointed to a door at the end of the platform.

"Just a minute," I said politely.

I opened the door to the room he'd pointed at and entered. It was cold inside, refrigerated to keep the wines cool. Since there were so many different brands and sizes of bottles, I didn't know where to start. The door closed behind me. I panicked. Where was the light switch? What if I was locked inside? I groped my way to the door, and luckily, it was unlocked. I peeked out and saw the man still waiting. I finally located the wine and brought it to the counter and rang up my first sale.

I liked selling. I liked seeing the cash register fill with money.

I thought I had a handle on the liquor items, as I had memorized the names and located where they were stored. I was serving the customers efficiently until a woman, another old person, came in. She was African American, and her head was wrapped in a bandanna. She had no teeth. She wanted snuffs. I had never heard of snuffs.

"Could you tell me what they are?" I asked.

She bit down on her gums. Her lips pressed together in a line. I listened carefully, fascinated by her toothless mouth as it explained to me that snuff was chewing tobacco. She described the jar. "It's a small brown jar and on the bottom are four small bumps in each corner." She said it was important that there be four bumps. Together, we found the jar. Sure enough, I could feel the four small round protuberances in each corner of the jar.

Now I added chewing tobacco to my knowledge base, committing it to memory. The whole time, Mr. L's roving eyes watched me like a searchlight in a prison. Since I was the first point of contact for customers entering the store, I was always alert to their queries. Many wanted to know where to find some specific piece of merchandise, and I could answer them.

Then one day, a man came into the store and looked around nervously. He caught my attention. I asked, "May I help you?" in my public voice. He looked up at me standing on that platform a good two feet above him and asked, almost in a whisper, "What aisle are the prophylactics in?" Here was another kind of merchandise I didn't know. Pro-phy-lac-tics, four syllables, a big word. Must be an important item. I needed to consult with Mr. L.

I turned on the loudspeaker and said, "Calling the Manager. A customer would like to know which aisle has the prophylactics. Repeat, please respond as to where the pro-phy-lac-tics are." I triumphantly gazed down at the man, thinking how pleased he would be by my prompt response. He, however, was not smiling. He got as close he could and whispered, "My God, you are naïve!" He quickly turned and headed out the door.

I didn't know what had happened. I got back on the loudspeaker. "Manager, cancel the request. Thank you." Mr. L never brought the topic up. I wouldn't have known what to say to him. I didn't encounter the word "naïve" until college, and I didn't know what prophylactics were until even later.

I WANTED TO WORK more hours. Luckily, a fellow student's parents operated a laundry/dry cleaning plant. Besides their daughter, they hired us students to work at their establishment. Our job was to wait on the customers; that, I discovered, was the easiest job in the place. The adults performed the hard work of operating the washing machines, the dry cleaning machines, and the ironing apparatuses.

As soon as one entered the back room, the noise from machines drowned out all other sound. Hissing emanating from the ironing contraptions was no competition, but their rising steam clouded the entire area. The workers manning those ironing machines looked like they were hobbling around because of the heat. In actuality, they had to move precisely to keep the process moving.

The workers picked up a garment and, in one swift movement, placed it on the ironing machine. Then steam hissed out to iron the garment. Workers had to tend to each part of the process. Their movements were like a choreographed dance, their routine repeated over and over again for hours on end. The rising steam, the accompanying hissing, and the rhythmic movements of these workers/dancers. Sweat poured down their faces, but their hands were too occupied with other tasks to wipe away the rivulets of perspiration. Their clothes stuck to their bodies. Left, right, turn around, bend, reach, off, on—I was in awe of how hard they worked.

I felt guilty about my job at the front counter. The most unpleasant part of it was sorting the soiled clothes. After I witnessed what went on in the back, I appreciated my counter job even more. In fact, I enjoyed "taking in" the laundry. One particular customer was mine: whenever he showed up, I was the clerk designated to wait on him.

The first time this man came in, another clerk, an African American boy, had waited on him. The customer was Asian, a small, bespectacled man in a dark suit with a starched white shirt and a tie.

"I wahntoo pheexoo duh buttonu onu pocketo," he said as he held up a white shirt.

The clerk said, "Excuse me? Can you repeat that?" He didn't understand, but I understood the Japanese man's sentence perfectly. He spoke just like my mother would have if she had known that much English.

I stepped in and said, "He wants to fix the button on his pocket."

His name was Yamashita. The clerk had to ask him how to spell the name. That was tortuous. "Y-aee-emoo-aee-esoo-echee-iee-t-aee." In the mid-1950s, there were no household Japanese names like Datsun, Toyota, Honda, or Mitsubishi.

From that day on, I became Mr. Yamashita's personal clerk. Conducting business with him was very formal. I was polite and so was he, but he did not become one of my favorite customers. I think it was because he was Japanese and I was sure he knew that I was not. Over the years, I had heard many stories of atrocities carried out by Japan when it annexed Korea in 1910. Koreans like my mother who had endured those harsh times harbored animosity toward Japan and its people.

BY MY SENIOR YEAR, our life in America felt comfortable, in the sense that there was a predictable rhythm to our daily living. Both my mother and I went about our respective routines and felt settled.

Being a student was my most important duty. I studied and studied, and then studied some more. In English classes, we read *Beowulf.* It was written in an English that I didn't know. Then came Shakespearian plays, written in another convoluted English that I had to decipher. I enjoyed learning. I wanted to excel.

Each day after school, I walked to the convent and practiced on the harp. I allotted an hour a day, but often my practice sessions went longer when I felt I hadn't mastered the assigned pieces. I asked Sister Noel at my weekly lessons to double my assignments. I wanted to make sure I didn't waste my mother's hard-earned money.

In the spring of my senior year, I had an added incentive to practice. One day, Sister Noel said she wanted me to prepare for a solo recital. She had been in contact with the nuns at Mount Saint Mary's College in Brentwood. She wanted me to apply for admission.

"You will be auditioning for a full music scholarship," she said. I could tell by her demeanor that she was excited. Normally, Sister Noel had one temperament—placid. Even conducting a cacophony of a beginning orchestra, she was calm. But that afternoon, she was chatty, smiling—she even had color on her pale face.

I was overwhelmed at the news. For the first time, I studied her with admiration and gratitude. Her long black robe covered her from her neck down. Only her thin face framed by the fanlike wimple and her small, veined hands were visible. I smiled at the memory of our earliest meeting. She and

I were at eye level when I was fourteen. In my senior year, I was two inches taller. She was petite in stature, but to me, Sister Noel was a giant.

We planned my audition. "I think the recital should extend for an hour. Let's start with a harp piece," she said as she made notes in her notebook. We sat in the alcove with the harp.

"In the middle of the recital, you will play the piano. And you will end the program with a medley on the harp. How does that sound to you, Joanna?"

"That sounds good, Sister." I would have done anything she suggested. My heart raced at just the thought of an hour-long solo recital.

We chose the music I'd play and developed the program. I had already memorized the pieces. She copied the title of each piece in sequence in her curlicue handwriting into my blue notebook. When she handed it back to me, she said, "We will work from now on to make these pieces a natural extension of you."

Sister Noel was a magician. I don't recall if she was ever annoyed with me. I do remember displaying temper tantrums when I became frustrated with particularly difficult sections. She had a knack of suggesting different techniques that I might apply. She tolerated my childish outbursts.

Sister Noel was the school's entire music department. She conducted the orchestra, and she also taught each individual student how to play his or her instrument. I even had an opportunity to play the trombone. Sister Noel instructed me on how to hold it, how to pucker up my lips, how to move the slider. Then when the instrument was positioned just right, she said, "Blow." Blow I did. So hard that I saw stars before me. I almost keeled over. It didn't help that the instrument was so heavy. I gave it up after one try.

Besides orchestra, she taught the glee club, choir, and chamber music group. Nevertheless, she remained the most even-tempered teacher at the school. I wanted to be in all of her classes. I practiced the organ so that I could be a church organist. I accompanied the choir at the High Masses, and I enjoyed playing at Requiem Masses and weddings. I loved the rich, full sound of the organ. When I played the organ in the loft of the church, I felt like I was at the threshold of heaven.

How did I manage to get into the choir? I must confess it had more to do with Sister's kindness than my ability to sing. After I auditioned, she said I should concentrate on playing the harp and piano. I pleaded with her. "Puh-lease, Sister. Puh-lease let me be in the choir." After many entreaties, she finally relented. Looking at me with her soft gray eyes, she said, "Joanna, you can be in the choir only if you promise me you will just mouth the words." I asked her what she meant. She said, "Don't sing aloud. Just pretend you are singing." I was so happy to be in the choir, I didn't even think "mouth the words" was insulting. I was ahead of my time and became good at lip-synching!

The day finally came for my recital. It was my day. For this special event, I wore a lace dress accessorized with a pearl tiara and a pearl necklace that I bought from Woolworth's. The entire student body attended. The school's auditorium was filled with students from first grade to twelfth grade. I peeked out from behind the curtain as they filed in by grades. With the nuns as teachers, even the first graders knew to be quiet.

Three nuns whom I didn't recognize sat in the first row. Next to them was Sister Noel. I opened the curtain a little more to look for my mother. She sat by herself in the last row of the auditorium, wearing her Sunday church suit and hat.

This was the first time she would hear me play the harp. The thought made me happy.

This recital was a culmination of what my mother and I had worked for since coming to America. I played with all my heart and soul, each piece like a stepping stone to our American Dream. Just as Sister Noel had envisioned, the music, the instrument, and I were one. Not until I muffled the remains of the last note, dislodged the harp from my shoulder, and gently set the instrument down on its base did I become aware of the applause. I walked to the center of the stage and bowed. The audience continued to clap. I bowed again.

Afterward, Sister Noel introduced me to the nuns from Mount Saint Mary's College. Meeting them made me nervous. I couldn't help thinking, did I pass the audition?

My mother stood at the back waiting for me. I went to her and took her hand. "I want to introduce Sister Noel to you, Omai." We waited until Sister Noel was alone. Upon seeing us, Sister smiled. I introduced my mother. Ever the proper Korean, my mother lowered her eyes and bowed to Sister. Sister then asked me to translate how pleased she was to meet my mother.

In reciprocity, the Korean protocol dictated that bountiful praise and gratitude be bestowed on Sister. Holding the Sister's right hand in both her hands and still with her head bowed, in her mellifluous tone, my mother declared in Korean how grateful she was and how indebted to the Sister for teaching her daughter. My mother used many flowery words to convey this message. Without taking a breath, and still holding Sister's hands, she told me to translate. I looked sweetly at Sister Noel and said, "My mother thanks you from the bottom of her heart for teaching me to play the harp." I wonder if my mother noticed how short my translation was.

I knew Omai was proud of me because she omitted the customary protocol noting how unworthy the recipient is of the patron's generosity. I was surprised yet pleased that she did not reference me as her "undeserving daughter."

Before my mother left, she complimented me. "You played beautifully. I think everything was fine." Then she frowned and added, "I did notice one thing. Couldn't you keep your feet still?"

My poor mother! She had never seen a harp and didn't know it has pedals that a harpist moves to change to a flat or sharp note. I could well imagine the anxiety of her not being able to tell me to keep my feet still.

IT HAD BEEN EIGHT years since my mother and I sailed under the Golden Gate Bridge to live in America. In June of 1959, I graduated from St. Agnes High School. Together, my mother and I achieved our first American Dream.

MOUNT SAINT MARY'S COLLEGE

M Y HEART THUMPED WHEN I saw a fat envelope among other mail in the mailbox. It seemed like an eternity since my recital. I had been waiting for a notification from Mount Saint Mary's College. I picked it up and placed it on the palm of my hand and bounced it in the air to assess its weight. I pondered whether a fat letter was a good sign or a bad one. I was scared to rip it open.

I carried the letter as if it were fragile. Once inside my house, I slit the top of the envelope with scissors. My mouth dry, my hands sweaty, I took out the contents and opened the folded letter. I read the first paragraph. I reread the paragraph, just to make sure. The only way I could tamp my pounding heart was to press my letter of acceptance from the college to my heart. I was admitted to Mount Saint Mary's College with a full scholarship! I couldn't wait to tell my mother. I looked at the wall clock. Two more hours before she would be home.

Two weeks later, another letter came from the college inviting incoming students and parents to an orientation at the campus. I don't recall the specific details of how my mother and I managed to travel all that distance to Brentwood from

South Central Los Angeles. We didn't have a car, and we did not know how to get to Brentwood on public transportation. Most likely, Sister Noel once again had come to my assistance.

What I remember about the ride was how the car had to wind uphill around and around so much that I felt nauseated. Throughout the drive, I prayed we'd get there before I threw up. Finally, we approached the driveway to the campus.

The first sight of the campus made up for the torturous trip. Perched on top of the Brentwood hills, the setting looked like an artist had painted the landscape and magically snapped his fingers to turn the painting to life. Framed by colonnades with high arches, the grassy open spaces with manicured gardens led to buildings crowned with red clay tile roofs. I was reluctant to walk on the clean pavement.

A student guide took charge of us. She smiled and introduced herself. She would be a senior in this coming year. With her clear voice, she informed us that the college was founded by the Sisters of St. Joseph of Carondelet. After an overview, along with the other prospective students and parents, my mother and I followed our hostess on a tour. Everything was beautiful. I especially liked walking under the long porticoes with their columns of ornate arches. With each arch we passed, I feasted on a new vista.

It was a sunny day, and a slight breeze fanned the abundant leaves of stately trees, gently tousling the guide's brown hair when she turned around to address us. The others in our group appeared so comfortable—parents whispering to their daughters, some holding their daughters' hands. They joked with the guide as if they already knew her. My mother and I trailed behind without talking. Amidst the beauty of the campus, the day, the event, self-doubt lurked in my mind.

After the tour, I had a private appointment with the Music Department faculty. My mother and I were the only guests. Not having had much social interaction outside of school and a small circle of Koreans, I felt ill at ease. The three Sisters whom I met at my recital rushed up to greet us. I noticed that these nuns wore their own style of wimple and robe. They clasped my clammy hands. When they turned to shake my mother's hand, I did have enough sense to introduce my mother. She, wearing her respectful face—eyes cast down, lips slightly curled at each end—grasped each nun's extended hand with both of hers, bowing simultaneously. Observing my mother's warm gestures somehow viscerally affected me as if she were caressing my hands also.

I politely answered all of their questions. Throughout our interview, my mother, dressed in her Sunday suit, assumed the subservient pose she had perfected. She stood with her hands folded and her eyes downcast, a hint of a smile on her lips. When necessary, I would translate for her. Then, she'd nod to indicate that she understood.

The nuns invited me to an impromptu jam session. A quartet—a cellist, a violinist, a flutist, and a harpist. The three nuns and I situated ourselves in a semicircle and played. Playing the harp finally made me feel at ease. I was a part of the music and a part of a quartet. We played until each one had performed a solo piece. When we finished our mini-performance, everybody clapped, including us, the performers. For the first time that day, I smiled. My mother watched, standing in her humble pose.

After we were served refreshments, the nuns bade us farewell. I took my last look at the campus. From where I stood, I saw the Pacific Ocean. I felt joy at the sight of the vast blue vista, as if I had encountered an old familiar friend.

THAT EVENING, AFTER THE dishes had been put away, my mother sat across from me at the kitchen table. I turned down a leaf of the book I was reading.

"What does Omai think about the school?" I asked in Korean, addressing her in the third person as a sign of respect.

"Jo-woon haek-kyo gah teh (It seems like a nice school)," she replied. She had brought her sewing basket. She picked up a spool and unwound the blue thread from it and snipped the thread with her teeth. She wet one end of the thread so she could guide it through the needle's eye.

She put the threaded needle down and looked at me. I sensed she was gathering her thoughts. "It seems like a nice school"—the watery sentence echoed in my mind. She rarely expressed her opinions with a subjunctive verb.

"I saw you playing the harp with those nuns," she said as if she was reminding me of some event that had happened a long time ago. I waited for her to continue.

"I saw your future at that moment." She picked up the threaded needle and tied a knot at the end. "If you go to that college, you will be surrounded by those nuns and indoctrinated by them. You will end up becoming a nun yourself, just like them."

My mother looked sad, which revealed her thoughts. She picked up a piece of underclothing to mend. Her eyes cast low and the right side of her mouth skewed downward. I could hear her sigh.

I let her remarks simmer. My mother knew me well. I strove to be a good person, a good Catholic. I paid attention in all my classes, especially the religion class in the first period. The nuns taught that they were married to Our Lord, Jesus Christ. Since, as a girl, I couldn't be a priest, becoming a nun was my only way to be the ultimate Catholic.

I wanted to be a nun. No, I needed to be a nun. Sins I'd committed weighed heavily in my thoughts. Every Saturday, I went to confession equipped with two, sometimes three pages of sins I had committed since the Saturday before. I had even devised a matrix to keep track. I listed the Ten Commandments on the vertical line. The horizontal line was divided into mortal and venial sins, sins of acts and impure thoughts, and how many times I had committed each sin.

I had spent a long time in the confessional, reciting each sin, referenced by which commandment I broke, the gravity, type, and frequency. Poor Father Ryan, my confessor! By the time I finished reading from my list, he'd give me absolution and penance and say, "Go in peace, Joanna" before he slid the little door between us. I hated that he knew who the sinner was. Then, I'd be sorry because "hate" is a sin.

Once when I went on too long in confessing my sins, Father Ryan interrupted and said, "There are no new sins, Joanna." That made me feel good because I thought I was the only person who invented new sins to sin! It was no wonder that my mother knew I would become a nun.

I waited for my mother to continue. She didn't ask me any questions. She held my gaze and said, "You will just be eighteen years old this year. You have your whole life ahead of you. If you go to the 'Mountain' school, you will be a nun for the rest of your life. I think you should go to UCLA." She held my hand in hers and softly added, "After you graduate from the university, if you still wish to be a nun, that's the time . . ." I filled in the rest of her sentence, "to decide," in my mind.

My mother, my rock, my everything! I trusted my mother's judgment. There was no question about obeying or not obeying. At that young age, I complied without giving any thought to the matter. I enrolled at UCLA because my mother decided I should do so. Life was simple then. Honor thy mother.

I DIDN'T THINK ABOUT our pivotal conversation on that evening until my mother died thirty-seven years later. After her death, in the process of uncovering my mother's life experiences, I learned the depth and complexity of living a life. My mother was right. Without her loving guidance, my life would have been irrevocably altered. At age eighteen, my life was only a prelude.

PART 3

AFTER OMAI'S DEATH

LAST BREATH

California, 1996

I NEVER KNEW MY mother could speak English in full sentences until January 17, 1996. That early morning, the telephone by my bedside shrilled. The ringing pierced my slumber. Oh, my God, I thought. The hospital!

I grabbed the phone, knocking the base off the bedside table. "Hello?" I could hear my heartbeat in my ear against the receiver.

"Hello. My name is Dr. Darnell. May I speak to Mrs. Choi's daughter?"

"This is her daughter. Is anything wrong?"

"Your mother's condition has changed for the worse. I think you better come over to the hospital right away." His voice was too quiet. The fluorescent numbers on the clock illuminated the room. I reached for the quilt crumpled on the floor.

"I'll be right there." Panic cluttered my mind. I couldn't think. I sat on the edge of the bed, still gripping the phone until the incessant buzzing sound coming from the receiver brought me back to my senses. My mother was dying. I had to go to her. I had been her ears and voice since she and I came to America forty-five years ago. Now, she needed me more than ever.

I took the shortcut. I could drive from my house to the hospital in twenty minutes if I ignored the speed limit. I knew the route from many previous emergency trips. The red light at Barton Road stopped me, but I kept my eye trained on the signal. The second the traffic light turned green, I stepped on the accelerator.

When I arrived at my mother's room, two residents were hovering over her. The small room was much too quiet. The young doctors were absorbed in studying her chart. My mother was hooked up to a monitor that constantly displayed spiky lines. The doctor who had called me said that her body was shutting down. I couldn't comprehend what he said. Or maybe I didn't want to acknowledge, even to myself, that I understood.

I fumbled to her bedside. She appeared to be sleeping. I was afraid to wake her up—afraid that I wouldn't be able to wake her up.

"How is Omai feeling?" I didn't know what else to say. My voice sounded like someone else's.

She opened her droopy-lidded eyes and gazed at me.

"Gwen-chan ha (It's all right)," she said softly and em-phasized her words with her trademark blinking of the eyes. Gwen-chan ha. I wanted to underline that sentence. Her pale face and matted hair, sunk so deeply into the pillow, gave me no reassurance.

She grasped my hand to scoot herself into an upright po-sition and looked straight at the two physicians who were now standing by the foot of her bed. When she had their at-tention, she touched her chest with her other hand and said, "I want to die."

The doctors and I stood motionless and speechless. My mother again tapped her chest with her free hand and re-peated, "I want to die." It must have taken all her energy to speak. She closed her eyes, still holding my hand. Her breathing was labored.

My heart raced but I felt numb. "I want to die," she had uttered. Not "I die," as I had expected of her English. In all our years in America, she'd cobbled English words together into sentences devoid of tenses and syntax.

I wasn't prepared for her to say a perfect sentence in English, much less for what she said. She must have known that I, her daughter, would refuse to translate her message to the doctors.

I looked at them with teary eyes and a quivering mouth. I felt helpless. Dr. Darnell came close to me and said, "Not on my watch." I wanted to believe his words with all my heart.

I somehow managed to get through the rest of the day, suspended from time and in a state of disorientation. My mother lay there in her hospital bed. The only signs of life were the slight rise of her chest that accompanied her breath and the neon lines displayed on the monitor. My heart fluttered with every bleep, followed by spikes and waves of lines across the monitor's graphs. In the darkened room, I peered out the small window that framed the infinite blue sky. Waiting.

From the hours that followed, I retain only fragments: listening for changes in her breathing; greeting my niece, Fran; embracing my son, Eric; the priest administering the last rites: a slow-motion movie.

Even the hospital staff's query as to where to send the body didn't penetrate my psyche. Like a robot, I said I would go home to retrieve the documents from the Forest Lawn Cemetery where she would be interred.

When I left her room, it still seemed as if my mother would hang on until my return. I drove home, glancing in the rearview mirror from time to time at the lowering sun and thinking I needed to get back before it set.

The phone rang just as I entered the house. It was Eric calling from the hospital, telling me that my mother's end was near. And that's when I knew. I was going to miss my mother's final moment. I barely remember rushing back to the hospital. I only know I was on the road and the setting sun was painting the sky with fire-red brilliance at 5:05 in the afternoon that January day when my mother took her last breath. She willed herself to die.

JUST YESTERDAY, LIFE HAD still seemed safe; the hospital routines provided a sense of continuity to normal daily existence. Yesterday, my mother, a self-reliant and independent person, was still sitting instead of lying in a hospital bed. Yesterday, she was still insisting on getting herself to the restroom rather than using a convenient bedpan. I had expected no less from my strong-willed mother.

Just yesterday, my mother sat in the only chair with arms in her green hospital room. I sat on the edge of her bed. The attendant brought her dinner tray and set it on the narrow adjustable table. My mother said, "Thank you," but she didn't even glance at the tray.

"Omai has to eat," I told her. "How about some applesauce?" My words were in Korean except for "applesauce," as I did not know the equivalent Korean word.

"Maybe I'll try it—just a little." She smiled at me. I peeled the foil cover off the cup and set it in front of her. I watched her eat—just a little, as she said. She put her spoon down and said, "Go-mahn. (Enough.)" She pushed the tray to a corner, tidying up, a habit of hers throughout her life. She looked at the clock on the wall and then turned to face me.

"You must be tired," she said. "Why don't you go home?"

"Ah-nee. (No.) I am not tired. Let's get the other things done." I was avoiding eye contact with her. I was tired, but I didn't want to leave her.

The last rituals for the evening were to take her false teeth out and put them in the blue plastic container to soak for the night. I picked up a small bottle of lotion from the welcome basket and asked, "Shall I apply this on Omai's legs?" She nodded.

I crouched and massaged her swollen legs. She watched me in silence. I cried in my heart as my hands held each tiny foot. When had she shrunk so much that she looked like a doll perched on a large chair?

I helped her onto her bed. She wriggled up to the top until her head reached the pillow. I pulled up the safety guard-rail. She looked at me standing there by her bedside.

"Zho shim heh. (Be careful.)" Her usual parting sentence, words I had heard thousands of times, just as familiar as her words of greeting: "Have you eaten?"

"I will come early tomorrow. Sleep well, Omai."

Only yesterday, that had been. How I yearned now for yesterday.

OMAI'S BURIAL

I RECALLED READING AN old proverb: "No girl becomes a woman until her mother dies." I agreed. Even at age fifty-five, I was not ready to become a woman. My mother and I had not finished our conversations. Unfinished conversations are like musical notes of an elusive melody playing over and over in one's mind.

The creaking of the mechanical gears interrupted my thoughts. I watched the men lower her casket into the ground. Like the incomplete melody, my mother's voice could no longer sound anywhere except in my mind.

The small group of mourners surrounded the gaping hole into which the casket was being lowered. My body witnessed the event but my thoughts were mired in all the unanswered questions being buried with her. Puzzles and questions about our family, which had been festering in my mind like sores throughout my life.

Whenever I brought up the past, my mother had one of two responses. Either she would wave her hand as if she were shooing away the topic and say, "That's ancient history." Or, if I pressed her, she would reply, "I don't remember." Then she'd close her eyes as if this gesture put a period to the conversation. I would set my queries aside for another day because back then it seemed there would always be another day.

The casket touched the ground with a thud. The sound brought me back to the scene. Big Brother was taking photos. I narrowed my eyes to focus. Was he really taking pictures of our mother's descent to her final resting place? My seventy-one-year-old brother, himself an old man at this point, had flown sixteen hours from Japan to attend his mother's funeral.

He had not changed much since I had last seen him, over a decade before. His hair was thinning now, but it was still jet-black. A short man, he stood erect. Too erect, as if he might fall backward. He reminded me of a penguin, even by his clothes. Every day, he wore a black suit, white dress shirt, and a tie. On prior occasions, he'd have two cameras strapped across his chest—one for black-and-white photos and the other for color. Today, he was making do with one.

Seeing him click away, I found myself puzzling over my mother's relationship with her firstborn son, especially in view of the culture from which we had all emerged. In Korean culture, the first male child is entitled to the top position in the family hierarchy, with accompanying filial obligations to his parents. I found myself wondering now: where was he on New Year's Day, all those years?

On New Year's Day, my mother would always dress in her favorite Korean garment, a pale-yellow silk blouse with indigo blue trim at the neckline and sleeves, and a long flowing skirt of indigo blue that matched color of the trim. She had her hair coiffed. She darkened her sparse eyebrows and put on lipstick for this special occasion. The only incongruity in her regal appearance was the orthopedic shoes with braces peeking out from her skirt as she sat in her faded purple velour-covered wingback chair.

Each January first, she would unwrap the fuchsia-colored silk cushion from an old sheet and place it on the floor about a yard away from her chair in her small living room. Seated there, she waited for friends and family to come by and wish her a happy and healthy new year. This was one holiday when she insisted that we adhere to the traditional Korean custom of kneeling on the cushion and bowing to her. All those New Year's Days, she waited for a call from her firstborn son. The telephone by her side never rang.

Equally confusing to me about their relationship was my brother's comment when I called him at another time of crisis regarding our mother. My second brother had died in 1979, and after that, with my first brother living abroad, I had felt like an only child in my relationship with my mother at times. Over the years, she and I changed roles; she became like the child and I became her custodian, except that she retained full authority over me. Sometime after her second son died, she had a stroke. She survived but was in the hospital for the entire summer that year.

Taking care of her took a toll on me. I yearned for support. In my most trying time at the hospital one evening, I called my older brother. I didn't even bother to calculate the difference in time at his end. I was desperate to unload my troubles.

He answered the phone. At the sound of his voice, I blurted, "Obba (Elder Brother), this is Joanna." With his usual formality, he asked, "Ah, Joanna. How are you? And how is Mother?" He pronounced "Mother" as "Mahthah," English being his fourth language.

As if his question had turned on a spigot, I poured out all my worries. He listened without interruption. I finished by telling him about our mother's declining health. Then I waited for my Obba to comfort me. I cannot recall what he said, other than the last sentence.

"Call me when something more definitive happens."

His words haunted me. Did he mean "definitive" as in "death"?

The sentence echoed in my memory for years.

Now, he peered at his mother's lowered casket. There was nothing more to do or say after the picture-taking. Only a handful of guests stayed for this part, the rest having left after the service at the church. My brother walked over to me and said, "Woon Ki's plot is near here, isn't it?" He surveyed the hillside.

"Little Brother's spot is up there." I pointed to my second brother's final resting place, about nine yards up the slope.

My second brother was Omai's favorite child. He was a handsome and charming man. My mother's face would light up at the very sight of him. Among her three children, he was the one who could really make her laugh. Often, they sat in the kitchen sharing secrets. They were mother and son but they were also best friends. He died in his forties and Omai never recovered from his death.

Seventeen years ago, it was my first brother and I who buried him. I remember asking my mother about attending the funeral. The two of us were sitting in the kitchen facing each other, and she just kept wiping the top of the table, which was already so clean one could eat off it. Over and over, she moved the dishrag in a circular motion.

I watched her hand, not knowing how to salve the pain she was suffering. Abruptly, she stopped. In a quivering, soft voice, she said, "Moat gah." Two words: "Can't go." Her eyes filled with tears. I understood her overwhelming grief by the way she took that limp rag and sat there wringing it again and again.

My mother never visited her second son's grave, although a few years later, she asked me to make the arrangements for her to be buried near him. That was so many years ago. I was not prepared for this day, now that it had finally come.

The two of us, my brother and I, picked up some of the bouquets of flower from our mother's grave. We walked up to our brother's grave. Over the years, the shiny marker had tarnished and gotten covered with wayward crabgrass. We placed the fresh bundles of flowers there. We had our photo taken: on either side of the marker, we stood like two dead trees. The picture captured the relationship I had always had with my brother.

I watched him lost in his own thoughts and wondered what he was thinking. All I had were unanswered questions. The questions I had shelved for my mother and me to talk through someday.

THE DREAM

Six weeks after my mother died, she visited me in a dream. In that dream, she, my son Eric, and I were in her apartment, in the living room with the familiar gold-and-black-striped velour couch against the wall and her faded wingback chair placed at a right angle to the couch. My mother and I were our present ages, but Eric was a small child. In actuality, he was in his twenties.

My mother sat in her chair as usual. She told me to check out something in the bedroom. This request was quite normal, as she frequently relied on me, especially in the later years of her life. In my dream, I would have done anything she asked, since I was so happy that she was alive and I had a chance to speak with her once again.

Eric, the little boy, said, "I don't like strokes." As dreams go, I accepted the time and sequence warp as natural. All that mattered was being with my mother. I knelt next to her, and we embraced once again, my flat chest cushioned in her ample bosom.

"Nah, Omai sahrang heh (I love you, Omai)," I said. I felt her embrace tighten. That dream was so real that in the dream itself I saw myself awaken. In that transition from dream state to wakefulness, I realized the meaning of my mother's visit. Time and language were irrelevant to this gestalt of understanding. Just as in our life together, my mother came to assist me on the path to healing. She knew how much I loved and missed her.

Omai must have known she didn't have much time left. A month before she died, the two of us sat in her living room at dusk. She sat in her wingback chair with her open Bible on her lap. Her eyes were closed but she still had her glasses on. When I crept to remove her glasses, she must have felt the nearness of me. Eyes still shut, she said, "I don't know how I am going to leave you. You will want to see me so much."

Bo-goo-pah (wanting to see someone) is the Korean expression for missing someone, longing for someone. I understood that in coming to me in a dream, she was telling me to live my years on this earth fully and completely. She visited me so that I would let her go.

But it didn't work. Missing her and letting her go simply did not go hand in hand. As days became weeks, I caught myself saying, "Now what, Omai?" like I used to say in my childhood. Like a child, I was mad at her for dying. If she hadn't died, I wouldn't be in this shape. Memories still raw inside me prompted me to question why and what if.

Several months before her death, my mother underwent an angioplasty performed on her right leg. When she and I had our initial consultation with the surgeon, I found myself disliking him. He rushed through our appointment. He sat in his swivel chair, tapping his ballpoint pen on his desk while I translated his words to my mother. It took time for me to describe what the angioplasty procedure was, as I didn't know the equivalent words in Korean. Her decision would be based on my translation. It had to be accurate. Seeing him checking his watch didn't help me find the precise Korean words.

I nicknamed him "Napoleon" in my mind: he looked like the movie version of Napoleon Bonaparte, a short, stout man strutting with splayed legs. My dislike of Napoleon turned to anger after the surgery, when the leg he operated on became infected.

The open wound on her right thigh oozed with pus. The visiting nurse instructed me on how to clean and dress it. My mother sat in her wingback chair. On the side table next to it, I assembled all the needed items: a large surgical dressing (8" x 10" sterile gauze), packets of smaller pads (3" x 3" sterile gauze), individually packaged saturated swab sticks, surgical tapes in their blue dispensers, surgical scissors, and a tube of prescribed ointment. Sweat smeared my forehead and the area above my upper lip. My mother must have seen the fear on my face.

"I can clean it," she said as she bent to unbutton the bottom buttons on her housedress.

I looked at the raw flesh, the size of a nickel coin. I had a sharp pain in my head just thinking about sticking a long swab stick in that wound. My mouth filled with sour saliva. I gulped it down. How my mother, my patient, endured the ordeal, I'll never know. It was a testament to her fortitude.

Months went by, but the wound would not heal. At the last appointment with Napoleon Bonaparte, I lashed out at the surgeon: "Well, you could now carve another notch on your bedpost! This time for operating on a ninety-year-old woman!" I didn't wait for the doctor's response.

"Omai, oori-gaja (Omai, let's go)," I said as I helped her up from the chair. I didn't need to translate. I sensed she understood what I had said. After all, we had been communicating without words all of my life.

Now, I wondered if my broken heart would ever heal. And I also wondered: what if she hadn't gone through with that procedure? What if we'd had a better surgeon? What if I had been a better daughter? Would she still be alive?

NEW YEAR'S EVE, 1995

NOW THAT SHE WAS gone, I couldn't stop brooding about the relationship between my mother and her elder son. In my earlier childhood memories, my mother's world revolved around Big Brother. Growing up as her makneh, her last child, I sensed Big Brother was an important somebody upon whom the entire family doted. Whenever he was around, I felt like a byproduct, a peripheral nobody.

This feeling went back to my earliest childhood days, when Big Brother didn't live with us. He attended boarding schools from elementary school through university and visited during holidays. When he came home, the entire household of my maternal grandparents catered to him, especially our mother. Indeed, my mother's daily routine was dedicated entirely to serving him. Three meals a day, she prepared his favorite foods. Every day she got up early and went to the kitchen in the courtyard, where she gathered kindling near the hearth of the stove and started a fire. She fanned the sparks until the blue flame turned orange-red. Then, the cooking began.

When my brother sat down at the table in the common room, my mother brought a tray containing a covered rice bowl, soup so hot that you could see the steam rising, and an assortment of side dishes. This was breakfast. The beginning of the day's food fair. She'd kneel close to the table and watch her son eat, always alert, replenishing his dishes before he asked. This pattern repeated at lunch and dinner, except that, as the day progressed, the meals got fancier.

I don't recall if Big Brother played with me when he visited. What I remember about him were stories my mother told me over the years, during my childhood. One story she repeated so many times imprinted him in my mind like a face on a coin. I had been a year old and my brother was studying for the entrance examination to a prestigious university in Japan. My mother always reminded me that at that time, when Japan occupied Korea, it was difficult for Koreans to get accepted into Japanese universities.

Her storytelling began after dinner, during a lull from a busy day, with evening chores yet to be done. She sat on a cushion with her legs tucked to one side and began.

"One evening, I slid the door open to your brother's room to ask if he wanted something to eat. You see, he had been in his room all day after eating his breakfast. He had given strict instructions that he should not be disturbed. But I thought he might be hungry. When I peeked in, what did I see?"

She looked at me with her eyebrows raised. I looked at her without guessing. Then, satisfied that she had my attention, she continued. "There he was—strapped to the back of the wooden chair with his belt!" She slapped her right thigh with her hand.

At this point, I knew to blurt, "Why did he do that?"

"So he wouldn't fall in case he dozed! I asked him if he wanted food. Without looking up from his book, he said, 'No. Eating will make me sleepy.'"

My mother paused to make sure her son's words sunk in. After enough time for reverential reflection for his words of wisdom, she continued. "On his eyelids he had smeared

Mentholatum ointment—thick enough to be visible from the door."

Again, I asked, "Why did he do that, Omai?"

"So he could keep his eyes open! Mentholatum has a strong medicinal smell. I imagine it stung his eyes. When I entered his room, it was freezing cold. I asked him if he wanted more heat. In those times, we had an ondol floor, which was covered with many layers of oil-glazed paper. The ondol system of heating provided heat from underneath the house. In some places near the heat source, the intense heat below would turn the covering from yellow to brown.

"He didn't even look up. He said, 'No. I don't want to get sleepier.' He kept up this regimen until he had memorized the entire Japanese-Korean dictionary, front to back. By the time he finished studying, he had lost all his hair."

Each time she ended this story by saying, "He passed the entrance examination, scoring the highest mark. Just think! He beat the Japanese in their own examinations! He was number one." My mother stuck her right thumb straight up.

My mother framed a black-and-white photo of him in his college uniform and displayed it prominently on a wall of the common room where nobody could miss seeing him. The picture was fixed to the wall but those beady eyes of his followed me whichever way I moved.

He left Korea for Japan when I was two and attended Kumamoto University for two years until world events intruded. In 1945, Japan surrendered, paving the way for the independence of Korea.

"The war was over and the Koreans had to leave Japan," Omai explained. "Your brother was at the train station. Everybody was pushing and shoving, trying to board the train. When he got to the door and was about to board, the conductor barred him from entering." My mother stopped and took a breath. "He didn't know what to do. He was upset that he couldn't get on the train because no one knew when or if there would be another train coming."

She fell silent and looked out the window. I waited for her to continue. I enjoyed the suspense she brought to her stories.

She turned her head and our eyes met.

"That train blew up. It was your brother's destiny that he was not on that train."

I had goose bumps, every time, listening to this story. I thought, Big Brother is someone very special!

I could picture her bright eyes and wide smiles as she told stories of her son. I could still hear her trilling voice and visualize her gestures of thumbs up for number one and slapping her thigh to note a physical exclamation point. How proud she was of him.

But that was long ago. Over the years, Omai stopped telling those stories. Eventually, it was as if she had locked them away deep inside herself and thrown away the key. I did not know why. But I wondered about it at times. I thought of the year she had her stroke and what Big Brother said when I called him, looking for sympathy and support: Call me when there's something more definitive.

Omai's final New Year's Eve was in the year 1995. Since her angioplasty, her medical problems had become more complicated. With New Year's Day looming, I was grateful the visiting nurse stopped by in the afternoon of New Year's Eve. The hospital had assigned us a Korean nurse, and the two of them chattered away in their native language, as I sat there, an observer, not a translator.

That evening, my mother watched TV from her wingback chair. Suddenly, she clutched the armrests. "The room is spinning," she said. I shot up from the couch and went to her.

"What's the matter, Omai?"

"Gah-mai-ee-so. (Be still.)" She closed her eyes tight. The front of her blouse heaved in rhythm with her short breaths. This was no time to keep still. I dialed 911 and the fire truck came in no time flat. Two strong paramedics attended to my mother, gentle giants, so calm, so efficient. They took her to the emergency room at the local hospital, and I followed.

The ER doctor attended to my mother and admitted her for observation. At 11:45 p.m., I said goodnight to her. When I reached home, the kitchen wall clock displayed 12:08 a.m. It was the beginning of a new year, and I had not even thought to stay with her until midnight to wish her a Happy New Year. Slowly I sat down on a chair at the kitchen counter. My body slumped. The only sound in the silence of the house was the ticking of the clock.

My thoughts traveled to our earliest years in America, to Los Angeles in the 1950s. On New Year's Eve, my mother would go to Mr. and Mrs. Kim's house on Jefferson Boulevard to join the other Koreans for a party. Everybody called the Kims' residence "The Club House," using the English words. Every New Year's Eve, my mother would say, "Mak nyahl eun nah neun Club House eh gahn dah. (On the last day, I am going to The Club House.)" She didn't need to tell me because I knew how much she looked forward to the last day of the year.

Weeks before, in preparation, she would replace the yellowed collar of her Korean blouse with a crisp white one. The replaceable collar is actually a border to the collar, a narrow strip of white silk. She sewed it on so perfectly that it looked like the fabric was glued on. Year after year, for that one night, my mother looked regal.

I tagged along when I was younger but stopped when I was old enough to stay at home. Over the years, it became a joke between us. I, the young person, had no place to go on New Year's Eve. It was my mother who danced and sang and welcomed the new year.

Now, in 1995, I wished I could transport her to those yesteryears. That night, I lay my head on my arms, unable to sleep, worrying about what this new year would bring. The next day, I brought my mother home from the hospital, relieved that she was discharged. Unlike other New Year's Days, when she would put on her Korean costume and sit like royalty in her wingback chair, she had to lie down. I helped her to her bed. Slowly she lowered her upper body to the pillow while I lifted her legs onto the bed. With her legs curled in a fetal position and her right arm under the pillow supporting her head, she lay on her side, hugging the edge of the bed.

"Have you spoken to your brother?" she asked. I hesitated before I answered. I had called him. Our conversation had been as disturbing as that earlier one years ago. I tried to think how best to relay what my brother had said this time.

"Yes," I said finally. "I called him. He is very busy with grading papers as final examinations are taking place. He told me to tell you that he'll come to visit you in February."

My mother took a deep breath and closed her eyes. I stood by her bed, waiting. She said nothing.

"Shall I call him again?" I asked. I knew she understood what that question meant. Did she want me to call him because time was running out? She let the question linger in the room.

Then she opened her eyes, those sad eyes hooded with droopy lids. She did not look at me; instead, she looked in the near distance as if she could see the endless horizon. "Don't call him," she said. "He is not my son."

She turned her body to her left side, facing the wall. The afternoon sun streamed in between the slats of the venetian blinds. I closed the blinds and smoothed out the comforter, lightly patting the contour of her small body. I needed to touch her to reassure myself that she was still there. I stood at her bedside in the quiet room with silent tears streaming down my cheeks. I felt helpless.

Reading my mother's gestures was second nature. When she faced the wall, it meant our conversation was over. She never explained why she uttered those words, nor did I ask. I heard the words she spoke, but I did not understand them: "Don't call him. He is not my son."

Did I do wrong in calling him after she died? Why did I call him, against her wishes?

Truth be told, I don't remember calling Big Brother. But I must have called him. Who else would have? Perhaps I called him because I didn't believe Omai really meant what she said. I could still see, in my mind's eye, Omai crouching near the low table replenishing her son's food after waking at dawn to heat the ondol floor for him. She loved her son. Perhaps I called him because I needed him to assuage my loneliness, for us to mourn our mother together as brother and sister.

I did disobey my Omai. But despite whatever thoughts and feelings had prompted her to utter those words, I hoped she would forgive me and approve. I could visualize her crooked smile and imagine her saying, "So he showed up after all!" Yes, her firstborn son paid his respects.

TIGER'S CUB

Los Angeles, 1951

MEMORIES ARE GOVERNED BY narratives we can't always see. Some are forgotten for reasons we can't fathom. Some are buried and then emerge, seemingly at random. One such memory that emerged: when my mother and I came to America, we didn't go directly to the Korean Senior Center. We went to Big Brother, who was living in Los Angeles at the time. It would have been only natural that we go to him, since, in Korean culture, filial duties fall upon the eldest son.

How we got from the port in San Francisco to the city of Los Angeles where Big Brother lived, I don't remember. Probably we boarded a bus. If so, it must have been a grueling all-day journey after our long sea voyage. We must have been exhausted as we climbed the stairs to the second story of the apartment building where Big Brother lived. We lugged a black cardboard suitcase packed with all our worldly possessions. Omai knocked, Big Brother opened the door, and we entered his small apartment. I have no clear memory of what happened next. That day and the days that followed are like one of those dreams that evaporate as soon as you open your eyes in the morning. I have no memory of how we greeted each other, what we talked about, or what we ate. I only know that I was once again what I had always been when Big

Brother was present: I was the gong-dai, the tail, attached to Omai. I followed her around and my prime duty was to stay out of the way, cause no trouble.

Big Brother had not known we were coming. He had not invited us to stay with him. Throughout my life, he was a stranger. I had seen him when he came to visit during school recesses, but really I only knew him as a photo on the wall. When he opened the door, the photograph came to life, but familiarity with the photograph did not prepare me for the man.

Neither of us knew how to talk to the other. We had never lived together, and there was a sixteen-year age difference between us. We had no basis for becoming friends. He was quite unlike my second brother, Little Brother, who had helped raise me and who had always kept in touch with me, even though his life had taken him far away from ours. Little Brother was eight years older than I, but we were close. He was the brother I went to for comfort and advice.

During our stay with Big Brother, Little Brother was away at school, boarding with an American family. I wrote to him often, saying how much I missed him and how much I wished he were with us. "Things would be so different if we were living with you," I wrote. "Little Brother would buy me things and not be so cheap like Gome." Gome means "Bear." It was a nickname Omai had bestowed on Big Brother, and in our letters, Little Brother and I used that nickname for our elder brother. His proper title, the one my younger brother should have used, was Kun Hyung: "Big Brother." As a younger sister, I should have referred to him as Kun Obba, which also meant Big Brother. But no, in my letters to Little Brother I had written, "I wish I were living with Little Brother instead of with Gome."

I don't know how long our stay with Big Brother lasted. It might have been weeks? I don't think it could have been months. One evening we had sat down to dinner. It was not unusual for the three of us to eat in silence. Big Brother packed both cheeks with food and chewed methodically and slowly until his cheeks deflated. Then he stuffed more food in his mouth, like a chipmunk. I never knew what he was thinking, as he hardly ever said a word to us. When he finished his dinner, he left the table and sat in a chair to read reports he fished out of his attaché case. My mother and I cleaned up.

At bedtime, Omai and I were lying side by side in our double bed when Big Brother knocked on our door. Without waiting for a response, he opened the door.

"Are you already asleep?" he asked. I knew he was addressing our mother, because he was using formal Korean. Our mother sat up. I lay still.

"This letter is from Woon Ki to Woon-hee," he said. At the mention of a letter from second brother to me, my heart skipped a beat. My right arm covered my eyes. I took a peek, still pretending to be asleep.

Big Brother shoved the letter at our mother.

"Why is it open?" she asked, as she ran her fingers on the cut side.

I am in trouble now, I thought.

I tried to keep my eyes closed but my eyelids fluttered like a hummingbird's wings. My heartbeat kept pace with my quivering lids, except louder.

"Because I thought it was to me," I heard him reply.

Sure, he did! My two brothers and I have the same first names but the second names are totally different. It would have been very difficult to mistake one for the other. If he was telling the truth, he must have been in quite a hurry. I pretended to be in a deep slumber.

Big Brother had paused. My mother waited.

"Did you know that she has been writing about me to Woon Ki?" From the crook of my elbow, I saw his sharp eyes boring into her.

My mother unfolded the letter from her second son and glanced at it. The thin paper shook in her hands. She said nothing. She was waiting.

I knew the content of my letter. I could feel Big Brother's anger. I wished I were dead.

"I am raising a tiger's cub." After uttering that statement, he turned and left. The bedroom door closed. I was doomed. I stiffened my body and prayed for death.

A bear raising a tiger's cub! I thought of this incident forty-five years later as we stood by our mother's grave. How little had changed! I was middle-aged now, but in his presence, I still felt like a ten-year-old child who couldn't keep her eyelids from fluttering no matter how tightly she shut her eyes.

I probably contributed to our eviction from Big Brother's home, but in hindsight I can see that our days were numbered from the start. Our mother tried her best to cater to her firstborn son, but nothing she did could please him. One time, he invited several friends to dinner. My mother cooked a feast fit for a king, but did her son compliment her for a delicious meal? No, he criticized his mother in front of his guests. After they had eaten, my brother told our mother to bring them hot tea. She brought a tray with four cups. Each cup contained a teabag with just a string attached to it. She had removed the small square of paper attached to the string: she thought that was what she was supposed to do. I can still see my brother's furrowed brows as he pointed to the teabag and asked, "Where is the tag?" Omai apologized to the men and returned to the kitchen. I clutched the yellow balloon one of his friends had given me, relieved that Omai was the one in trouble, not me.

The final blowup happened when Little Brother came to visit us. It wasn't long after the greetings were spoken that the conversation among the three of them developed into a full-blown argument. I don't remember what it was about. Maybe I never really knew. One thing I can say for sure: it was mother and second son against first son. I hid in the bedroom, my heart thumping rapidly, wondering how it would all end. My second brother shouted an obscene word one day and stalked out. A week or so later, Omai and I found ourselves once again lugging our old black cardboard suitcase up a flight of stairs, this time to the front door of the Korean Senior Center. We rang the doorbell and that's when our new life in America really began.

MY MOTHER AND ME

Unryul, 1944

MEMORIES, AS I SAID, are governed by a narrative we can't always see. In the dark hours and days and weeks after Omai's death, questions I had suppressed for years filled my mind. So much had always been hidden in shadows. Always, I had thought that Omai would someday shine a light into those shadows for me. Now that Omai was gone, deeply submerged memories crawled out of nowhere to gnaw on my grief. And when these memories came into view, it was easy to see why they had been submerged.

When I was about three years old, my mother told me I was not her daughter. I don't remember what I did to make her say that, but most likely my infraction had to do with some act of stubbornness. As far as I can remember, no one, not even my mother, could make me do anything I didn't want to do. I probably exasperated her so much with my defiance that even when I had not done anything bad, she sometimes greeted me with the words "You, bad girl!"

In this particular instance, however, I must have done something really bad. "When you were a baby," she screamed, "I found you under a bridge. I should never have brought you home!" Upon hearing her words, my whimpering became a wail. I cried for the rest of the afternoon. I conserved my energy by droning when no one was nearby and wailing when family members walked past our open room. I had inched my body to the edge of our common room so that I had a full view of the goings-on in the courtyard.

Dinnertime came. My mother and Little Brother sat in the same room and ate their meal. They ignored me. I continued crying, alternating between droning and wailing. When there were no more tears, just a monotone humming sound coming from my mouth, I made myself cry by feeling sorry for myself for not having a real mother. Glazed with tears, my eyes followed my false mother's movements. I made myself cry louder when she came nearer.

The dusk turned to evening. I forced myself to drone but I couldn't keep my eyes open. The next thing I remembered was my mother talking. I lay still.

"She is not breathing!" I heard her say. "This girl is so tough she can breathe through her anus!"

"Is she all right?" I heard Little Brother ask.

"She's fine," she answered. "She is a yuh-woo (vixen)."

I lay there thinking that she was going to be sorry when I died. Tears welled up but I did not cry.

A BABY ABANDONED UNDERNEATH a bridge by a riverbank. I never brought it up, but now I wondered why she had uttered those words. Do other mothers say such horrible things to their daughters? That their daughters are not of their own flesh and blood but foundlings they retrieved from under some bridge?

Over the years, mixed in with both the good times and the hard times my mother and I endured, the most difficult were those we impaled ourselves upon. I cannot recall any single incident or action of mine that propelled my mother into rages, but I must have been very good at provoking her because she certainly flew into some epic rages. Every incident started out as an ordinary conversation. Some wrong word, some misconstrued phrase on my part, lit my mother's tongue on fire, and then it would begin.

"Yuh-woo yah! (You vixen!)" she would growl. In Korean, calling a girl or a woman a fox is a derogatory term, as it means an evil person. This would be followed by her recitation of my undesirable traits, the most egregious one being that I was an ingrate. I could handle her hurling of epithets my way, but not the imminent bodily harm. My mother would grab whatever was nearest to her. Unfortunately for me, she was always equipped, as she was rarely idle.

The scariest times were when she held a butcher knife. She'd stop cutting up a chicken and come after me with the knife held high, ready to chop me instead of the chicken. Once, she even charged at me with a hot iron. She held the iron like a shield while addressing me: "Jook il yuhn! (One who should be killed!)" I feared her, but each time she came after me, I escaped being slain. In those days of sorrow after her death, I found myself wondering: did I escape because she let me flee? Or was it simply that I could run faster than she?

ESCAPE TO CHINA

Pyongyang, 1930

THE DARK MEMORIES SURFACING unprovoked plunged me into a reexamination of Omai's life, and of our life together, and so, inevitably, into an agonizing reappraisal of myself. After all, what did I know of my own origins? Who was I? Where did I come from? Where had I been? From a lifetime of conversations with my mother, I knew that my family had fled to China, and I knew that they lived in Beijing for a time, but I didn't know much more about their stay in China. I didn't know why they were there or what happened to them there. It was only after my mother's death that I got a few details about that period, and what I got was scant because I got it from Big Brother, who was only five years old when the family fled Korea.

After Omai's death, we made an effort to stay connected. He lived in Japan but his work brought him to Los Angeles from time to time. On one such occasion, we arranged to meet at a Korean restaurant midway between the airport and my home.

Both of us arrived at the parking lot of the restaurant at the appointed time. He wore his black overcoat, now frayed, and his black fedora hat. We shook hands.

"How are you, Obba?" I asked.

"Fine, fine." Always two fines. And always the same protocol: I opened the restaurant door for him and he entered. Upon seeing him, the Korean waitresses bowed and led us to a table by the window.

I watched Big Brother finish his favorite lunch meal, naeng-myun. Seeing him eat, I recalled how our mother would put a large metal bowl of hot broth on ice to chill for this cold noodle soup. She'd pile the buckwheat noodles into the bowl and then, into her firstborn son's bowl, she would add a hard-boiled egg. I remembered these images from Unryul, so long ago and so far away.

He ate; I waited for an opening. After the waitress cleared the first dish and before she brought the next, I drew from my purse an old 3" x 4" photo that my mother had trimmed into an oval shape to fit into a now-tarnished metal frame. It was a family portrait with Father, Mother, Big Brother, Little Brother, and a young woman—before my time. My mother's hair was piled high and she was wearing a Korean dress. She sat in a chair with Little Brother on her lap. He looked about one year old. Sitting next to her was Father, also dressed in Korean garb. Standing behind the chairs were Big Brother, about nine years of age in the picture, and the young woman, who must have been the maid.

"Where was this picture taken?" I asked Big Brother.

He examined the photo for a long time, enough time for me to study him. My brother was an old man now. I could see where his comb had plowed through the now-gray strands on his head. His upper eyelids were swollen and red, hooding his cloudy eyes. The left pupil lay still. His wayward eyebrows, black and bushy, were the only remnants of his youth.

"This was taken in China," he said finally.

He took off his glasses, blew warm breath to fog each lens, and with his handkerchief, methodically wiped them. He inspected his glasses and put them back on.

"During the Japanese occupation," he said, "my uncle shot a Japanese policeman. If they had found him, they would have executed him, and not only that, they would have come after the entire clan. We had to leave everything behind and run." He stopped talking as if saying this much had exhausted him. Perhaps it was the jet lag; he had just gotten off a sixteen-hour flight from Japan, which is a long journey for such an elderly man.

But I was just getting started with my interview. My mother was gone, Little Brother was gone, there was no one left to help me fill in the gaps in my life story except Big Brother, and our visits were so infrequent, I had to get as much information as I could when I had the chance.

"How did you get to China?" I pressed. "And where in China did you live?" I sat with my pen poised over my notebook, ready to write down his response. I half expected him to brush me off, but he surprised me by asking for my pen and notepad.

He drew an outline of Korea and the border with China.

"Here is Korea. Seoul is right here—" He made a mark. "And north of Seoul is Pyongyang. Here. From Pyongyang, we took a train to Shieuju." He drew a line from Pyongyang to Shieuju. "Then, we went to Tandong."

I peered at the map he had drawn. Tandong is on the Chinese side of the border. He wrote Tandong in Chinese characters. He drew a line going north to Shenyang, made a circle and another line north to Harbin, and meticulously labeled each place.

"By Harbin," he said, "this is Sungari River." He drew two wavy lines from left to right to indicate the river. To the right of the wavy lines, which is to say on the eastern side of the Sungari River, he made a black dot. Next to this, he wrote Bao-Ching.

"That's where we lived. We lived in Bao-Ching." He put down the pen and took a sip of tea. "It was a two-day boat ride on the Sungari River from Harbin to Bao-Ching."

My brother handed me my notebook with his drawing of the map. I was grateful to him: I had now a faint intimation of the drama of my family before I was born, a faint sense of where I came from. The map was my very own treasure map—a map to the treasure of lost stories that were my roots.

At home, I took out my notepad and flipped the pages to the map. The family rode on a train from Pyongyang to Shieuju. I wished I could have asked my mother how long the train ride was and whether she was frightened. I wished I could ask her, "Omai, what was that train ride like, compared to the one we took during the Korean War? And was it winter when you crossed the Tumen River? How did you do it? Was the river frozen? Did you walk across the ice? Did you carry your son on your back, tightly bound to you with a ddee? Did you cross at night to evade the border patrol?"

As their escape unfolded in my imagination, I started worrying about it as if it were happening now and might still go wrong. I visualized my mother sitting on a bench with her young son sitting on her lap waiting for a train, in a foreign country, with no official paperwork, pretending to be just an ordinary family going to visit relatives. I had read that Harbin is called the "Ice City," as it gets very cold in winter, and I wanted to ask, "Omai, were you warm enough? It took two days by boat to reach Bao-Ching. Omai, did you have to wait until the river ice melted?"

I wondered how she must have felt, at age twenty-five, leaving her homeland, parents, and siblings to flee to China—with a five-year-old son. Did the young family of three—father, mother, and son—get away on their own or did they go with others in her husband's extended family? It wasn't as if they were going on a vacation. They were running from the rampaging Japanese conquerors who had invaded Korea! It would've been too dangerous for all of them to travel together. The clan must have separated into groups. It would have been the cautious thing to do.

OVER THE YEARS, WHEN my mother talked about her life in China, she had offered nothing of substance unless I asked, and even then, she'd answered only my specific questions. Our conversations turned into interviews. They didn't lead to the delightful storytelling sessions she was known for.

Growing up, I formed stereotypes of the Chinese from her stories. "The Chinese never counts his money in the open. He puts both hands inside his sleeves to count by feel. That way no one can see how much money he has."

"Chinese men never change clothes. In winter, they wear the same cotton padded blue jackets. They smear their snot on their sleeves so that the sleeves become stiff and shiny with green mucus."

I was impressed that my mother spoke not only Korean but also Japanese and Chinese. I asked her if it was hard for her to learn Chinese.

"No," she said. "I was young then, so it didn't take me long to learn. In fact, when I wore a cheongsam, the Chinese thought I was Chinese!" Her smile revealed how pleased she was to be taken as a native.

She told me that she wore the style that the Shanghai girls wore.

"The girls from Shanghai are beautiful—tall, lithe, and fair-complexioned, unlike the girls from the southern provinces," she said. The way my mother held her head high and poised, I could picture her as a Shanghai girl.

In our early years in America, we would treat ourselves once a month by going out to eat at Man Fook Low restaurant on San Pedro Street in downtown Los Angeles. My mother spoke fluent Mandarin Chinese, but unfortunately for us, the Chinese waiters spoke Cantonese. She tried to order the familiar dishes in Mandarin but the restaurant specialized in chop suey and egg foo yung. We ordered one item on the menu exclusively, two bowls of dumpling soup, man-tou soup in Chinese, man-doo soup in Korean. Invariably, after devouring her soup, she would say, in a low voice, "The Chinese food here doesn't taste as good as the food in Peiping." That was her signal that it was time for us to leave.

At home, my mother prepared Jah-jang-myeon, a noodle dish that originated in China, Jha-jiang-mian in Chinese. She made her own noodles out of white flour. The process took a long time from leavening of the dough, to kneading and flattening it with a rolling pin, to cutting it into one-fourth-inch strips. I was glad she never asked me to help, as I could see how labor-intensive it was. My contribution was to eat with gusto her homemade noodles topped with roasted soybeans.

But these were only glimpses into a life she had lived before I was born. I had so many questions about that life. Some I had never asked and many I had—that Omai had not answered. Why not, Omai? Why wouldn't you tell me what happened to you in China?

ANOTHER ESCAPE

Peking, 1932

"LITTLE BROTHER WAS BORN in China in February of 1933," my mother said one day, as she flipped the calendar page over to that month. "It was just after the Japanese attacked Manchuria, where we lived. I was pregnant with your second brother when we had to flee. I rode in a cart and the ride was so bumpy, I thought I would lose the baby!" She touched her stomach and smiled. "It's a wonder he was born so strong and healthy."

Only two years before that, my family had fled from Korea to China. Now they were in flight again. I knew from history what must have precipitated this second flight. Several months before my second brother's birth, the Sino-Japanese War broke out. The triggering event occurred in a city called Mukden, near Harbin, the town closest to where my family was living. The Japanese accused Chinese dissidents of dynamiting a section of railroad owned by a Japanese company. The Imperial Japanese Army invaded Manchuria and established Manchukuo, a puppet state of Japan, and in 1932, they occupied Harbin.

Once again, political upheaval had intruded on their personal lives. Once again, they had to flee, this time to Peking, or Beijing, as it is known today. During her lifetime, what I was able to piece together of my mother's life in China was as crude as a child's painting. It's as if I took a large brush and splashed onto a canvas a yellow circle for the sun, blue for the sky, green for grass. I couldn't make out the foreground that had taken place against the generic background of history—the story in which my own life was one small thread.

Over the years my mother offered only snippets. The family had so much money in China that they stacked wads of paper money from wall to wall and measured the height with a ruler in order to count how much they had.

Once I asked her about a prominent angry scar on her right side, and she said her husband had fired a gun and the bullet ricocheted and hit her. She delivered this news blandly, as if she was just telling how her husband had swatted a fly. Had gunshots been a common occurrence in their household? She went into details about the outstanding medical treatment she received in Peking at a German hospital named after the Kaiser. It had been odd that she was so enthusiastic about the hospital and showed so little emotion about being shot by her husband. When I was young, I hadn't asked why he shot the gun.

Could that incident have been related to another story my mother shared with me out of the blue? One evening, she told me that my father and his colleagues smuggled yeh-pyun—opium—from China to Korea or vice versa. I visualized movie-like images in my mind when she spoke of sewing secret pockets in her husband's garments, of tense farewells in the middle of the night, waiting, always waiting and praying that he would come home safe. As the silent movie reeled on, I feared for my father. He must have felt like a tightrope walker. What if he was caught? He became a romantic figure, an adventurous man who laughed at danger.

Years later, when I broached this topic, she denied ever having said anything about opium. And I let her be. She was an old woman by then.

MY FATHER, THE
DOCTOR

I NEVER KNEW MY father. I cannot remember at what age
I first saw a photo of him. It had to be in America, for in
Korea, our life had been too hectic to daydream over photos.
Most likely it was after we had finally settled into the back-
house behind the senior center, where we had a bathroom
of our own and furniture bought from a nearby secondhand
store.

One day I went to Woolworth's to purchase picture frames
and a photo album. I wanted to organize the loose photos stuffed
in a well-worn envelope labeled in Omai's handwriting: sah-jin.
I scattered the photos on the kitchen table, and one of them
caught my eye. I waved it in front of my mother. "Who is this
man?" I asked.

"He is your father," she answered.

I studied his photo more carefully then. It was a black-
and-white snapshot of a young man with piercing eyes wearing
rimless round glasses. He sported a well-groomed mustache.
He looked dashing with his head tilted slightly to the left. The
man, forever young in the photo, didn't match my mother, who
was in her late forties.

"How old was he when this picture was taken?" I asked.

"He must have been in his early thirties." She continued to wash our dinner dishes and didn't offer to elaborate.

"What happened to him?" I was hesitant to ask because I didn't want to cause her pain. In my earliest years, I learned the word "gwah-bu" and knew she was a widow.

I studied her face but detected no change in her facial expression. After she dried her hands, she came to the table and tucked the photo in the envelope and sat down.

"We lived in China. He was a doctor. Actually, he did not have a formal education in medicine, but he learned it on his own. He opened an office. He had many patients and he was doing well as a doctor." She paused. She took a long breath.

"One day, he left for his office early in the morning as usual . . . He never returned home." And that was it. That was all she would say.

"Did he get to see me? Did he think I was ee-bbo?" The word has multiple meanings. Depending on the context, it could mean "pretty" or it could denote the verb "like."

My mother smiled at me and said, "Nuh, chahm ee-bbo dah goh heh." I couldn't quite make out the meaning of those words. Did they mean he thought I was very pretty? Or did they only mean that he liked me very much? I couldn't tell. Perhaps my Korean wasn't quite good enough.

"He was a nice-looking man," I said, as if I were commenting on a stranger. I felt sad for my mother. It must have been like living in limbo: all those years of not knowing if her husband was alive or dead.

The fate of my father was a mystery as far as I was concerned, almost like reading a historical novel, the end of which was missing. Given the Japanese invasion of China, he might have been kidnapped by the Japanese and forced to work for them. He was, after all, a doctor, even if self-taught.

Given that a war was raging, if he had been slaving for the Japanese invaders, he very probably did not survive.

Over the years, I thought about that stranger in the photo who was my father. How proud I felt that he was a doctor. Not only was he a doctor, he was a young and handsome doctor. When I grew up, I planned to be a doctor just like him. I daydreamed that someday he would show up at our doorstep and we would be together as a family. I daydreamed that someday I would finally be able to call him "Abuji."

One evening, my mother enhanced his image with an aphorism. I had said, "There are so many families with the names of Lee and Kim. Not too many with the name of Choi."

"Choi is a noble surname," she said. "There is a saying in Korean: 'Where a person whose name is Choi defecates, no grass ever grows on that spot.'"

She didn't need to elaborate because I knew it meant that through my father, we were connected to nobility. How fortunate I was to be a Choi and to come from such a potent lineage!

But all the snippets from Omai didn't add up to a coherent picture. There were too many missing pieces, too many questions and contradictions among the pieces. Many pieces didn't seem to fit yet boldly demanded inclusion in the portrait of the woman who had given birth to me. Who was this woman, my Omai? In search of answers, I would take my own fateful journey to the East.

PART 4

RETURN TO ASIA

THE JOURNEY BACK

May 1996

S OMETIMES, WITHOUT KNOWING IT, you're straddling a chasm. It might happen between two breaths as you're feeding a spoonful of Jell-O to your mother. That's how it seems to me now, looking back at that moment when time and space were suspended and my mother was hovering on the verge of death. I was feeding her yellow Jell-O, I was fluffing her pillow, I was monitoring the spiky lines on the neon screen, I was just a hamster on a wheel, going and going—numb to awareness of any chasm.

But my mother knew. After she had taken that last swallow of Jell-O, as I was wiping her mouth and smiling and feeling pleased that she had eaten the entire contents of the little plastic cup, she helped me across the chasm. Sitting upright, with two pillows behind her back, she said, "Back in Korea, when a person dies, that person's clothes are burned so that her spirit has clothes to wear in the afterlife."

I was speechless. At that moment, I remembered a particular outing when I'd been a toddler riding on her back— my mother had carried me on her back everywhere then. We passed a hillside dotted with perfectly shaped mounds. "Omai," I said, pointing. "What are those?"

She had stopped. "That is where our ancestors are buried."

Now I understood: after my Omai died, I would have to return to the land I had not seen in over forty years. I would have to go back to Korea.

IN PREPARATION FOR MY trip, I picked out three of Omai's favorite pantsuits. They were lilac, apricot, and gray—her favorite colors. I wrapped each set in white tissue paper before I placed it in the cardboard suitcase she had bought with Green Stamps back in the 1950s. Although my mother was buried in America, the burning of her clothes, the Confucian ritual, should be carried out in her motherland.

Korea had been a single kingdom when she was born. I had checked an old map and located the village of Unryul, where my mother's family lived for many generations—and where I'd lived with them as a very young child. But I couldn't return there: it was located in Hwang Hae Do, a province of North Korea.

My mother had been the fourth of eight children: Neh-chai, "Fourth Child." She had left all those siblings behind when she fled North Korea at the age of forty, but she preserved memories of their time together and until her death fifty years later, told me stories about their childhood years together. One sibling, however, she rarely mentioned: her oldest brother.

Being the firstborn son, that brother inherited all of the family's landholdings. He was a schoolmaster, and in Korea in the 1920s, being a schoolmaster was a highly respected post. I wished now that I had paid better attention to the few details she had dropped about his life. I got the feeling she was not fond of him. Whenever she referred to him, her mouth twisted downward. She chewed her spit as if it were bitter-tasting. "He didn't care about his relatives," she said.

"All he cared about was his immediate family, just his wife and his children. His wife could crush him just like she'd crush an ant with her thumb. He was not a man."

Nor did she have much to say about her two other older siblings. They must have died in childhood, since she was the one who took care of the youngest siblings—two girls and two boys.

One of her younger brothers fled to the south when Korea was divided, leaving his wife and children behind in what became North Korea. Like my mother, he had a crooked smile. When I was a seven-year-old child, I remember him smoking one cigarette after another. My mother covered for him by saying he smoked only because he missed his family and couldn't get a job. Eventually, his wife and their two daughters fled from North Korea and joined him, and they had a life together after the war. He was gone now, but I would visit his widow on this trip to South Korea.

I don't recall my mother's two younger sisters. I must have met them when we lived in North Korea, but I knew of them only by old photographs my mother managed to bring along when we escaped from North Korea.

Her favorite brother was the youngest. When she talked about him, her face beamed like sunshine. "My youngest brother is so handsome. He has big eyes. Now, there is a real man." She had raised him like her child, and in all those fifty years of exile, she missed him the most. After we left North Korea, she had seen him, a soldier in the North Korean army, only that once, during a brief ten-minute visit in the middle of the North Korean invasion of Seoul, in 1950. That had been my only glimpse of him. She replayed that ten minutes in her mind over and over again in the remaining fifty years of her life.

I was anxious to talk with my aunt in South Korea, who was now my oldest living relative. Which siblings were missing? What happened to them after 1950, when the Korean War erupted? That was the last time my mother had any news of her siblings and relatives in the North. Did my aunt know anything about their fate? This journey would not just be about burning my mother's clothes. This was a quest to know myself.

VISIT WITH BIG
BROTHER

Japan, 1996

M Y HUSBAND, LEE, AGREED to accompany me. Our journey to Korea would take us through Japan, where I had been only once, in 1951, when my mother and I were fleeing war-torn Korea, headed for America. With my mother's death still raw, I was oozing grief and regret, and the thought of Japan had a lifelong bitter taste, the seeds of which had been planted in my great-grandfather's time, when the Japanese conquered Korea and during their brutal thirty-five-year occupation committed countless despicable acts. The Mansei story I had heard from my mother became emblematic of Japan for me. I could never erase the image of that girl whose insides burst when the Japanese police thrust a fire hose deep into her vagina and released a torrent of water.

Tucked away for half a century, that story flashed into my mind on the fifth of May, 1996, when the plane I had boarded in Los Angeles touched down at Tokyo's Narita Airport. We could have skipped Japan and flown nonstop to South Korea, but my older brother, the only living member of my immediate family, was teaching at a Japanese university. Having lived the first twenty years of his life under Japanese rule and having been educated in Japan, he was just as familiar with Japanese culture as with Korean. Given his looks and mannerisms, he could in fact have passed for Japanese. The Koreans are generally taller than the Japanese, but not my brother: he was short of stature. His eyes had that thick epicanthic fold typical of the Japanese. Bowing came naturally to him; he had an entire repertoire of bows for different people and different circumstances, just like a native Japanese. At age seventy, he divided his teaching between two universities, one in South Korea and the other in Japan.

Our plane landed at 4:30 p.m. It had been a long flight in a cramped seat, and I had slept fitfully. My elder brother was waiting for us at Exit 1, wearing the same suit he had worn to our mother's funeral four months earlier, or one just like it. I saw him as my husband and I walked out of the restricted area, and I waved. My brother nodded.

When we reached each other, my brother and Lee shook hands. "How was your flight?" he asked courteously. Waiting next to Lee, I was not sure what to do: should I hug my brother? Shake his hand? Kissing him never entered my mind.

He made the decision for me, by reaching out for a polite handshake. "How are you, Joanna?" At that moment, I had a kindly feeling for him. Here he was again in real life, a living, breathing human being, and not the photo that had hung on my mother's living room wall.

My brother, I soon discovered, was all business. With the greetings out of the way, he transformed into our tour guide. He led us out of the airport, which was no small feat, for Narita is one of the largest and most congested airports in the world. He walked fast for an old man. Lee and I were pulling our heavy luggage and could barely keep up.

We headed for the train station and joined the people queuing up in single file at the designated boarding place: my brother, my husband, and me, in that order. The train was already full of commuters when it arrived, but we managed to squeeze in. We were lucky to find individual seats. My brother sat on one side, Lee and I on the other. Young people stood. No one spoke. The compartment was packed but silent. The only sound was the whirring of the bullet train. Many people had their eyes closed, and most of the others read newspapers. I peered out the window, fascinated with the glimpses of urban landscape zipping past: towns with gabled-roof houses and narrow alleys. Sporadic fields of vegetation.

Just when I started to doze, my brother alerted us that we would be getting off at the next stop. There, however, we merely transferred to another train, and then transferred to another before finally reaching the town of Kawagoe on the outskirts of Tokyo.

From the train station, my brother led us to a hotel. It was a modest one catering to local clientele. Patrons' shoes were neatly lined up at the entrance. My brother spoke to the clerk and returned with an envelope containing a key. He led us through a dimly lit corridor to a room that was small and clean.

"Leave your luggage here. My wife is preparing dinner for us at our apartment. To get there, we must take the train for two stops," my brother said. He had a Harvard accent—as in "Hahvahd." My brother was used to people obeying, and we did not fail him. We followed him out of the hotel and back to the train station. An old Japanese man bowed to Lee as he stood waiting for the train. In this small town, the local people probably didn't see many foreigners. A tall man with blue eyes and almost white hair was bound to stand out.

We alighted at Kamigaseki station and my brother again led the way, winding through dark, narrow alleys. "Here we are," he said. "This is where we live." The apartment building had two stories. We walked up to the second floor.

My sister-in-law opened the door. I had known On-nee since I was seven, when she was already in college. My mother and her mother had grown up together in North Korea; our families were from the same province. My sister-in-law was quite the opposite of my formal, distant brother. She was a gregarious person, always ready to share a good story. She laughed easily and it was hard to see her eyes when she did, so crinkled was her face. Her wide smile pulled her eyelids taut toward her temples.

"Ah! You are here!" she said in accented English.

"Hello, On-nee. How are you?" I replied. We greeted each other with words only, which is not unusual for Koreans, who are more accustomed to bowing than hugging. I scanned the place. There were two small rooms. The entrance room, which had a kitchen with a mini-sized sink and mini-sized appliances, also served as a living and dining room. The back room was their bedroom, with a tiny bathroom attached. In Japan everything was small.

On-nee set the low dining table with all my favorite food. Bulgogi, jap-chae, and kimchi. I inhaled the familiar, pungent smell of marinated barbecued meat. I hadn't eaten these dishes since my mother died. Tears welled in my eyes, and I felt a lump in my throat.

We crowded together at each side of the table. The men sat cross-legged on the floor. I sat with my legs to one side, ladylike, per my mother's instruction from long ago. My sister-in-law kept the conversation going while serving us. I nodded from time to time, but mostly I devoured my dinner. This was comfort food: my mother's food.

After we finished our dinner, the time had come to ask my brother my questions. I needed him to help me fill the gaps in my mother's history. I knew almost nothing of her life from 1905 to 1941, when I was born. I needed to know that part of her story in order to fully know my own.

My cue came when my sister-in-law got up from the table, gathered the empty serving plates, and took them to the sink. I reached into my purse for my 3" x 5" blue spiral memo pad in which I had written a timeline of important dates. I was expecting this to be easy for Big Brother: he just had to fill in a few factual details. It would be like coloring within the lines of a coloring book.

My brother covered his mouth and picked his teeth with a toothpick. I opened my notepad and held my pen poised, ready to jot down the important facts of my mother's life. I began by telling my brother what I did know.

"Omai was born in 1905. She married in 1924 when she was nineteen. The following year, 1925, Obba, you were born. Eight years later in 1933, Little Brother was born. She told me he was born in China while you all were living there. What I'd like to know is where did Father, Mother, you, and Little Brother live from 1933 to 1941 when I was born?"

He was silent. My sister-in-law, who was ordinarily so loquacious, so well-versed in anything and everything, quite suddenly seemed to have lost her ability to speak. She stood there holding a plate of sliced oranges. I waited, as it always took my brother some time to frame his thoughts. Time stretched on. What was his problem? It was a simple enough question: where did they live? That's all I was asking.

Finally: "We lived in China." He spoke nonchalantly as if he had said that it rained today.

I pressed on. "When did Father disappear?" As soon as I said those words, my sister-in-law placed the dessert plate down and went to the kitchen area, ten feet away. Apparently, she wasn't going to be a participant in this conversation. My brother assumed his thinking position, sitting like a Buddha in contemplation, or looking like a bear . . . everything about him was in slow motion. His eyes were downcast. His mouth was firmly closed. The small room, hot from cooking, suddenly felt cold. The heat had evaporated and condensed into a thick shroud of chilled air. I waited.

He looked up at last, his eyes shielded by heavy lids and thick glasses.

"Your father disappeared long before you were born," he said in a tired voice that was barely audible.

I was puzzled by his phrasing. Not *our* father, not just *Father*, but *your* father. Silence. Four people in a room, each with private thoughts.

Standing by the sink, my sister-in-law said, "Ask Victoria when you see her." Victoria was their daughter, whom I would see the next week in Korea. But I didn't want to wait until next week to ask their daughter a question that my brother could answer right now. Why was my sister-in-law handing the question over to her daughter? I ignored her comment.

I asked my brother again: "What year did he disappear?"

This time, he took even longer. "Do you really want to know?" he asked, almost in a whisper. Was he scowling? Or was that a worried frown?

"Yes! That's one of the reasons we made this trip."

"She wants to find her roots," Lee chimed in.

My brother took a deep breath and let it out. "After my father, who was a physician, left our house in Bao Ching, China, to make a house call, he never came back. He was carrying his physician's bag and was probably a target for robbery. Several days later, someone came to the house and reported that my father had been thrown into a well." He stopped.

I sat stone-faced, I imagine, visualizing a man at the bottom of a well.

"What year was that, and how was it that I was born in Haeju?" I asked.

Minutes passed. Heavy silence. My sister-in-law intervened.

"Who told you that you were born in Haeju?" she asked.

"My mother." Why was she asking that question?

Finally, my brother continued. "After my father went missing, Mother moved us back to Unryul, her hometown, where she bought land with the money left from her husband. We then moved to Haeju so that I could attend a secondary school. Mother ran a boardinghouse there."

I asked again. "What year did my father go missing?"

"Around 1936," he said.

His answer made no sense. I felt blood draining from my face. I felt lightheaded. There was nothing to hold onto, as a tingling sensation made my body feel like crumpled tissue paper—dry, fragile, lifeless. I was there and yet not there.

Everything seemed to stop except the thoughts that thundered in my skull with torrential force. My mother gave birth to me in 1941. My father went missing around 1936. Something was very wrong. This could not be. This would mean that my father was not my father. Then, who was my father? Where did I come from?

I don't know how much time elapsed. For the sake of the others, I composed myself. I breathed in and breathed out, slowly. I opened my mouth to speak. On my first attempt, no sound came out. I cleared my chalky throat and tried again.

"Who is my father?" I asked. My clammy cold hands shook.

My sister-in-law, who was still standing by the sink, addressed her husband. "I am ninety percent sure who the father was," she said.

I was a mere bystander now.

"I am one hundred percent sure," my brother said.

They were discussing the very core of my being in terms of percentages, speaking as if I were not even present. I managed to sit erect, my folded legs numb from sitting on the floor.

My brother spoke. "Your father's name was Hwangbo Do In. He was several years older than I. He was a boarder at my mother's boardinghouse." He said these shocking words in his usual unemotional, clinical manner.

My heartbeat thumped in my ears. Bewildering thoughts erupted in my mind. I could not stem them. My brother was sixteen years old when I was born. I added: sixteen plus three. The boy who sired me was nineteen when I was born and my mother was thirty-six. This could not be. I knew my mother. She would not—she could never . . . I was unable to speak.

Outwardly, I mimicked my brother's factual mien. I listened to his account as if I were a third party, unconnected to this sordid story. I was humiliated for my mother. All her life she had worn her widowhood like a crown. I should not know such a secret, not about my mother, my very proper mother.

I didn't want to know, but it was too late. Anger was welling up in me, anger at my mother. Here I was, mourning a mother who had betrayed me. My pounding heart kept pace with my roiling mind as I plunged into the cold currents of my mother's past.

As casually as I could manage, I asked, "Was he a class-mate of yours?"

My brother answered right away. "He was in his senior year. I remember him." He paused as if he was conjuring an image of that person. "Hwangbo," he added, "is not a common Korean name." He stopped and the three of us waited.

"Many years later, I met a fellow whose surname was Hwangbo. This was in South Korea. I was attending a meeting and happened to see his name tag. I asked him if he knew Hwangbo Do In, since the surname is so rare. The man said it was possible they were related."

I was imploding with emotions, but I had to pretend to be as detached as my brother, for his sake as well as mine. I continued asking my questions, carefully, as if I were stepping through a minefield.

"How did you know she was pregnant?" I wanted a nice answer: a foolish hope, given the horrible ending of this story, which I already knew. It ended with my birth. My brother seemed relieved, as he must have thought I was taking the news well. His answer came easily.

"I didn't know about her pregnancy."

I did not wait for him to elaborate. "How could she?" I spat the question to no one in particular, not knowing what the question meant, nor even if it was a question.

"She had her needs." That was my brother's answer.

My mother's indiscretion reduced to a single sentence. "She had her needs." It reverberated in my mind for the rest of the evening, aborting my recollection of the entire conversation: "She had her needs."

The answers I prodded out of my brother that night were pages torn from a story impossible to fathom. My mother became a stranger to me. I became a stranger to myself. The answers only provoked new questions, questions without answers. How could I not have known? What did my mother think? What did she feel about conceiving me with a boy not much older than her son? Did she suffer for her deed? Why did she never tell me? How could she have kept this from me?

That night, I lay in a twin bed in a hotel room in a Japanese town far away from my home in California, churning with thoughts more foreign and bizarre than I could ever have imagined. I tried to fall asleep but could only manage to pretend—for my husband's sake. The evening must have been difficult for him as well.

Finally, we gave up trying to fool each other. I checked the clock and saw 3:00 a.m. flashing in a green fluorescent glow. I pulled the quilt over my head, wishing I could turn time back to two days earlier, when I was in my own bed and my life story was still intact. Overnight, I had transformed from a grieving daughter to a bitter bastard child.

I turned to my husband. "You can't sleep either, can you?" I whispered.

"No. I was thinking of a movie I saw over forty years ago," he said.

I knew my cue. "What was it about?"

From his twin bed, cradling his head with his hands crossed beneath it, he recounted the story. His familiar voice was a salve to my raw senses. I closed my eyes.

"It was about a beautiful young woman who is married to a count. She falls in love with the gardener for the estate. The gardener is very gentle and handsome, but he is disabled. Theirs is a forbidden love, from which she becomes pregnant. Her husband believes it is his child. One day, when he's talking about the gardener, he lets slip an offhand remark: The gardener is impaired due to a rare genetic defect. At that moment, in horror, she realizes that her love affair may be revealed when the baby is born. Her whole life will be torn apart."

"And then what happens?"

"That was the last scene in the movie."

We lay in our beds, each with our own thoughts.

He summed up the link between what he recalled from forty years ago and now. "The aristocratic woman's status was ruined and her future—like your mother's—distorted as if by a curse." Without addressing me directly, he said, "In the movie, the genetic defect made the entrapment inevitable. In life, before abortion was legalized, many women's lives were destroyed by pregnancy."

I thought about my mother. How different would her life have been without me! Was her life irreparably harmed by my birth? The closure I had sought dissolved into questions. Questions I had never in my life anticipated.

PLAYING THE TOURIST

Tokyo, 1996

O N MONDAY, OUR FIRST full day in Japan, I woke up feeling brutalized. It was as if I had turned into an old woman overnight. But my brother had arranged for us to see some sights, so I suited up to play my role of tourist.

The four of us took the train to Tokyo for a morning of sightseeing. My brother wore his black suit as usual. My sister-in-law, at age sixty-eight, looked like a student with her blue sun hat and her small leather backpack. They walked fast, expertly navigating us to the world-famous Ginza.

We must have walked the entire length of that shopping district. So many stores selling electronic goods! How could they all stay in business? But for me all the shops blended together. All these sights and sounds of a bustling city registered as mere background noise. Struggling to cope with what I'd learned, I felt like a sleepwalker.

My thoughts drifted back to my last stop in Japan, forty-five years ago, when it was just my Omai and me. It was the first and only time we had flown on an airplane together. Omai appeared comfortable flying and I remembered mimicking her every gesture so that I would feel comfortable too. Sitting by the window, I saw spiky metal spears sticking out of the wing of the airplane. "Omai," I said, "what are those called?"

"Those are propellers," she answered. At that moment, the propellers began to move and my eyes opened wide as they turned into circular whirls.

We weren't in Japan as tourists then. We were in a desperate flight from war. Japan was just a gateway to America, to our new life. That much I understood, but at age ten, all I wanted was the red ribbons that adorned the hair of a Japanese girl I had seen walking down a street in Yokohama. Now, I didn't know what I wanted.

My brother hustled us to the Shiseido Parlor in Ginza for lunch. Adeptly, he ordered our food and resumed talking to Lee about the rapid rise of Japan as a global economic power. "Ginza is known for having the highest cost per square foot of land in the world," he said. I sat sipping coffee from a tiny cup and thinking, no wonder a cup of coffee with no refills costs five dollars.

The following day, my brother picked us up early. He brought three bento boxes, along with a six-pack of beer for himself and Lee. The three of us took the bullet train to Osaka. He procured a local guide for a private tour of a Shinto temple. In the afternoon, he took us to a river, where we boarded a boat. As he dispensed the tickets to us, he said, "From the boat, you can view the city from a different perspective."

A different perspective indeed. This man could plan our outings to the most minute detail and yet he couldn't even see me. Was I that good at pretending? Did he really think I was engaged in sightseeing? Could he possibly not see how far removed I was from the visual splendors of Osaka? Throughout the day, I marveled at my brother's demeanor, so engrossed in giving us a comprehensive tour, as if Sunday evening's revelations had never happened.

Big Brother and I had a sibling relationship in name only; he had always been the adult, I the child. It was no surprise that on these excursions, my brother spoke primarily to my husband, relegating me to the role of bystander. I was not surprised when I found myself offering to carry my brother's satchel packed with books. This was a little sister's duty. And I was not surprised when Big Brother accepted my offer.

On Wednesday, the three of us started early for our trip to Kyoto. I looked forward to the long train ride, as this would give me an opportunity to ask my brother about matters that had consumed my mind for the last three days.

As soon as the train left the station, a uniformed porter steered a cart down the aisle announcing, "Ocha, ocha."

My brother interrupted his conversation with Lee to say, "We will eat our breakfast now. What do you want to drink? Tea, coffee, juice?"

I broke in to ask my question. "You didn't know Mother was pregnant, did you?" My brother didn't look at me. He addressed his answer to my husband, as if it were he who had asked.

"I had no knowledge that Mother was pregnant. She had bound herself tightly and was wearing a very loose Korean skirt. One could not tell that she was pregnant." He took a sip of tea. "One day, she said she was going to visit some friends in Pyongyang. So you"—he locked eyes with me briefly—"were actually born in Pyongyang." He turned back to Lee. "About a week or so later, she came back with a baby girl. She said that she adopted the baby, as she did not have a girl."

My heart beat faster. "Was it possible?" For a brief moment, I tricked myself into thinking this might be what really had happened. She'd found me under a bridge. She'd saved me. This was a version I could accept. This story would exculpate my mother.

But Big Brother cut me off. "No. Everybody knew the baby was hers." He popped a piece of sushi into his mouth with his chopstick.

I didn't want to know any more, not until I'd had a chance to digest this distasteful information. But my brother wanted to tell Lee more, and even though I didn't want to hear the words, I was drawn into his story.

"Her liaison with the boarder was not a single occurrence. That woman was the proactive person." He spat the words "that woman," speaking of his mother. My mother.

I observed him clinically. What animosity this man, this son, harbored toward her. Clearly, her behavior had caused him extensive damage.

I understood now the years of noncommunication between mother and son. On the rare occasions when they met, they both went mute, weighed down by unspoken words stored from long ago. For decades, they had buried that long-ago event. And he was doing it still, burying that ancient secret under a charade of normalcy.

We arrived in Kyoto. My brother again assumed his role of tour guide. He translated the Japanese guide's words as we toured the Nejo Castle. And I, like a good student, wrote in my notebook: The Shogun used it for temporary headquarters while he visited the Emperor, while the capitol was in Kyoto. I took notes to keep my mind from straying into the awful thoughts churning inside me.

The next stop was the Golden Pavilion. We had our pictures taken in the typical pose, brother and sister standing erect and apart, like two sticks planted in the dirt. My brother made sure we saw all the important sites. In the afternoon, a bus took us to Nara. We visited the Deer Park, where deer were actually roaming among the visitors. The temple within the park contained a huge Buddha. Near it was a Shinto shrine with hundreds of stone lanterns. I wanted to pray for my mother, but I didn't know the Buddhist protocol.

Once that day, I thought I saw my mother—an old woman of my mother's build and stance, catching her breath. For an instant, I thought she was going to come to me, that I would once again hold her hand and hear her say, "Cham jottah! (It's wonderful!)"

There was a time when she could have been that old woman in this place saying, "Cham jottah!" Many years ago, my brother's immediate family planned to have a Christmas reunion in Japan. I thought it would be wonderful if our mother could join her son and his family. It had been a long time since she had seen his children and grandchildren. It would be an opportune time for her to make that journey. She was in her early eighties, and who knew what the years ahead would be like. The three of us were sitting in my mother's apartment—Omai in her wingback chair and Big Brother and I on the couch. I said to my brother, "Wouldn't it be nice if Omai could join your family in Japan?" Without waiting for his answer, I turned to our mother. "Would Omai like to go to Japan for Christmas?"

I waited for a response from either of them, but she just lowered her eyes. I thought she might be waiting for an invitation from her son so I turned to him. "What do you think, Obba?"

After a moment, he replied, "We'll see." Mother and son sat like two Buddhas in meditation. It turned out that "we'll see" meant "no."

At the end of a long day of our tourist charade, I was ready to board the train back to Tokyo. The incessant interplay between sightseeing and agonizing internal rumination had drained me. For the return trip, my brother bought another six-pack of beer. We sat in the same arrangement as earlier, with a table between us. My brother and my husband opened beer bottles, toasted each other, and guzzled the first bottles down. Even had I been a drinker, I doubt my brother would have offered me a beer. I closed my eyes.

The last conversation I overheard was my brother telling Lee that God had been good to him because he had done so much good for so many people. He held forth on his own generosity: he'd allowed our uncle and his family to live in one of his vacant houses in Seoul. My mother had told me a very different version of this story many years ago. I wished I could have shared with her the version my brother was now telling.

A BIRTHDAY PARTY

Japan, May 1996

NOVOCAIN COULD NOT HAVE numbed me any more than the shocking disclosures of that first evening in Japan. It was hard to believe it had been just five days since then. My brother seemed oblivious to the havoc he had caused. Each day he took us on another meticulously planned outing. Each day, the shell of me played tourist. Each day, some of the numbness wore off—until the evening of May 9th.

We were celebrating my brother's birthday. I knew his birthday was in May, but without my mother, I didn't know the exact date. In years past, my mother would say, "Today is Big Brother's birthday," circling the date on the calendar on the kitchen wall. "He was born in the year of the cow. People born in those years are hard workers, just like cows."

Now for the first time in my life, I was actually attending his birthday party. He was turning seventy-one and he had no appreciation for his good fortune: he'd had his mother for almost seventy-one years.

He and his wife picked us up for the celebration. He said he had invited the vice president of the university where he taught to join us. He gave us a neatly wrapped box and instructed us to give it to the vice president as a gift. He had guessed correctly that both my husband and I were ignorant of Japanese social protocol.

We went to a small restaurant tucked between shops. Three valances depicting cherry blossoms, done in silkscreen, decorated the entrance. They fluttered like flags as we ducked under them to enter. Inside, Japanese paper lanterns cast a warm glow while piped the recording of tinkly music played on a samisen.

My brother spoke to the hostess. She bowed, he bowed, we all bowed. She led us into a private room covered with a tatami floor. A long scroll with calligraphy writing hung on one wall. An Ikebana display, a simple yet elegant flower arrangement of chrysanthemums and pine placed in a turquoise vase, graced the low table. We removed our shoes and my brother told us where to sit. We three obeyed his orders and sat upon our individual cushions. He reserved the head of the table for the vice president. I twirled the tassels on my seat cushion while we waited for the guest of honor to arrive.

The vice president came bearing gifts. He was an older man, but not as old as my brother, and did not fit my stereotype of a Japanese man. He was tall, with an open countenance, and smiled easily.

We ordered dinner. The three men sat next to each other, the vice president at the head and my brother and Lee flanking him and facing one another. He did not speak English, but my brother was fluent in both Japanese and English, so the men were able to converse easily. My sister-in-law sat next to her husband, I sat to Lee's right.

The male camaraderie intensified as more rounds of sake were consumed. I watched, intrigued, as my brother poured sake into a tiny porcelain cup and handed it to the vice president. Usually, my brother sat waiting for others to cater to him. My brother raised his cup and toasted the vice president in Japanese. It was entertaining to observe the vice president's Japanese translated into English by my Korean brother so that my American husband could understand. Then the reverse—the American's English translated by the Korean to Japanese. I'd never seen my brother so verbal.

They shared more and more stories: three old men recalling WWII. Since Japan had allied itself with Germany, the vice president spoke German. My husband, of German descent, understood a little German. So German was thrown into the mix of languages in play. At one point, my brother turned to Lee and said, "We fought you in the war."

We? I thought. He thinks he is Japanese! One of Japan's goals during the occupation of Korea was to make Koreans into Japanese by edict. Koreans had been stripped of even their very names. It struck me now that my Korean brother was one of the most successful products of Japanese acculturation.

As Lee later pointed out, there's camaraderie among drinking buddies. This was the first time I had seen my brother less than serious. Along came another round of drinks, hosted by Lee this time. My sister-in-law and I ate in silence.

After dinner, we segued to a Korean karaoke bar next door. My brother led the way, the men first and we two women bringing up the rear. We climbed the steps single file to the second floor. The Korean hostess bowed to my brother, and they seemed to know each other well. She led us to a table. Unlike the Japanese restaurant we had just left, this place was dimly lit and more intimate. We settled into a private section. Stale cigarette smoke and a lingering smell of liquor permeated the place. In the dark I couldn't judge how well-worn the furniture was until I sat down and my knees popped up to my chest.

The hostess brought drinks. This time, instead of sake, hard liquor. The vice president and my brother must have been regular drinking buddies for quite some time, but my husband didn't have any trouble catching up to them. Fueled by alcohol, they were happy. More toasts. My brother joked: "Let's have another round. After all, a bird does not fly with one wing." I had never known this side of him. Soon the three drinking buddies discovered more common ground, singing German war songs. Even Lee knew these songs.

My sister-in-law, usually sociable, remained quiet. She and I were voyeurs. Against the backdrop of the men's joviality, my heart ached for my mother. The karaoke machine played a familiar song, one my mother used to sing, a song in an atonal scale with a melody that was so sad, so haunting. My brother started to sing along to "Shina no Yoru." At the sound of those lyrics, my tears flowed so suddenly and heavily that I could only see the others as distorted refractions.

I closed my eyes to dam the tears. In my mind, I saw my mother, her head tilted to one side, her eyes closed as if she were remembering a lover from years past, a secret she shared only by singing. And this was the song I heard her singing, in my mind.

The nostalgic melody infused me with sorrow. How she loved to sing and celebrate. Her son sang the second stanza. I wanted to shout: "Are you thinking of your mother on your birthday? Where is your tribute to your mother, the woman who gave you life?"

He sang the last stanza, sustaining the final note. So many birthdays our mother had, and had this son remembered even one? Not one card. Not one telephone call. She had kept all the cards she received in her lifetime. Only one postcard from her firstborn son. It appeared to have been sent from Washington, D.C., showing cherry blossoms in full bloom. There was no address or postmark, so it must have been enclosed in an envelope. On the otherwise blank back, she'd written, "1949. Wasn't that a long time ago?"

Lee touched my arm, puncturing my preoccupation with the accusations raging in my mind. Even in the dim light, he sensed my quiet volatility. He searched my face, touched my cheeks, and felt my tears.

"What's the matter?" he asked. I looked at him and more tears poured out.

My brother and the vice president were singing a duet to "Shina no Yoru."

"Son of a bitch!" I cried. That statement summed up my feelings as I struggled with the juxtaposition of my mother's death and my brother's birthday revelry.

Sadness, pity, and grief overwhelmed me. So did anger. Betrayal. Regrets. Love.

"Son of a bitch!" I bawled while the karaoke machine continued to play my Omai's song.

"You know, you were the tragedy that brought great disturbances to your brother's life," my husband said that early morning after the birthday party. It had become a habit for us to debrief in the quiet of the night back in our hotel room. We couldn't sleep anyway, due to jet lag.

Lee offered his analysis of my brother. "The shame he must have felt. Cut off from his friends. And of course, the tragedy of a lifelong, painful relationship between mother and son. It never got resolved. Sometimes unsaid words and stories are the most hurtful of all."

I lay on my small bed, looking up at the dark ceiling. Its blankness complemented our somber conversation. I was reminded of the confessional where I used to confess my sins, secure in obscurity. As if addressing my alter ego, I said, "Remember what I told you my mother said a few days before she died? 'Don't call him. He is not my son.' How she must have waited for him to call. It must have broken her heart to utter those words—'He is not my son.'"

"By choosing to keep you, she lost her son," Lee said. "I am sure she didn't anticipate that, but as the years went by, she must have thought, What have I done?"

My husband saw the relationship between mother and son from the perspective of the son; my empathy flowed to our mother. Softly, I said, "Is his treatment of her justified because of her indiscretion? Because of my birth?"

Lee remained silent. So did I.

THE NEXT DAY, WE departed for Korea. The five days we had spent in Japan felt like they had happened in slow motion.

Sightseeing was an art form for my brother. He proved himself an outstanding tour guide, but I did not want a tour guide. I needed a brother who would put his arms around me and console me as only a brother could. I looked at the green fluorescent numbers on the clock by my bedside table the morning we left Japan. Back in California, it would be a bright and sunny yesterday morning. Here, even though the sun was shining, it felt like night.

BACK TO KOREA

Seoul, May 1996

FROM MY WINDOW SEAT on the bus that would take us to the airport, I waved to my sister-in-law. I felt a momentary rush of warmth, seeing her standing on the train platform smiling and waving. But then, that was just how I had felt toward Big Brother six days earlier, when he greeted us at the airport in Tokyo.

My visit ended with no visible change in the relationship with my brother. We said our farewells in the same manner as our greetings six days earlier: "How was your trip?" he said when we had arrived, and "Have a safe trip," he said when we left. All was cordial and perfunctory. The revelation about the circumstances of my birth might as well have been reduced to ashes stored in some invisible jar inside my mind. For him, to all appearances, the conversation had never occurred.

Fleetingly, I even questioned whether that first evening's conversation had really happened; maybe it was someone else's horrible dream. Outwardly, the four of us erased it as if to protect the semblance of a family.

BUCKLED INTO MY SEAT on the plane bound for Seoul, I mulled over the words my mother had spoken in the hospital: "Back in Korea, when a person dies, that person's clothes are burned so that her spirit has clothes to wear in the afterlife." This last leg of my journey would take me to Korea to fulfill her last request.

When we landed at Kimpo Airport, I was struck by my own reaction to my native land. Everywhere Koreans were milling around, jockeying for a better look at the people disembarking from the plane, and they all looked alike to me, a homogeneous race. They talked so rapidly and with such accents that I couldn't understand them. I was one of them and yet, here in my homeland, I felt like a foreigner.

I looked around for Hong Bok, my uncle's eldest son, as we walked the path designated for passengers coming out of the plane. The other side of the roped area was filled with people waiting for alighting passengers. It didn't take long to spot Hong Bok, thanks to a 30" x 20" poster with our surname in calligraphy. Next to the pillar that displayed the poster stood two tall men with broad smiles. They looked like my uncle: they were his sons. They waved their arms in a wide gesture, and their excitement was contagious. I rushed to them and, forgetting protocol, hugged the one I got to first. His younger brother was waiting to be introduced; I hugged him too. I couldn't help it: I loved these cousins at first sight, they were my kinfolk, my connection to Omai.

Hong Bok took charge. He had even typed out a schedule for our sojourn here in South Korea—in English. He had made hotel arrangements, and he drove us there to check in. My husband thought that going to Korea would be an easy trip, not like going to Japan where I couldn't speak the language. He didn't take into account the fact that my use of Korean became stunted beginning at ten years of age. Koreans were surprised to meet a fifty-five-year-old Korean woman who spoke a childish, ancient version of the language in a Northern accent.

That evening, we were invited to dinner at Hong Bok's apartment on the outskirts of Seoul. The three-story beige building looked more commercial than residential. If it weren't for the laundry hanging on sticks from some of the windows, I would never have guessed this was an apartment building.

"Here we are," Hong Bok said as he opened the front seat passenger door. We followed him up three flights of stairs to his apartment. We took one step through the door and we were inside a small living/dining room with a sofa that could seat only two. My relatives were all standing, smiling: my uncle's widow, his three sons, his two daughters, and their spouses. The grandchildren lurked shyly near the adults. Everyone was there except the second daughter, who lived in the countryside—over a dozen people, all of them family.

My aunt rushed over and held my hands. She tilted her head upward to look at me closely. She held my gaze and spoke in her soft voice. I didn't catch her words but I felt the welcome and saw the tears glistening in her eyes. She turned to my husband and bowed and motioned us to the sofa. Once we were seated, all my relatives sat on the floor, looking up at us, still smiling.

I asked Hong Bok for the proper way to address his mother. Without my own mother to advise me, I was ignorant of the elaborate lineage designations. I learned that one addressed the wife of an uncle on the mother's side as Soong-Mo. I repeated the word to myself a few times before I used it formally to address my aunt.

The last time I had seen Soong-Mo was in Seoul in 1950 at the zenith of the war. Now, forty-six years later, I clutched her hands. My Soong-Mo, a small woman with strong big hands and gnarled fingers, must have been in her late seventies. Her tanned, wrinkled, round face was still pretty. I could imagine her as a young woman before childbearing and manual labor left their mark.

Hong Bok introduced us to his family: his wife and two sons and his older sister, Jo Sook, whom I remembered as a child. She used to have noodle-sized mucus constantly running down from her nostrils. Now, she was a stately-looking grandmother.

When my mother and I left Korea, my uncle and aunt had only two daughters. Since then, four more cousins had been added, and I had to work hard to memorize their birth order. Hong Bok, thankfully, introduced them in that order. They were such a warm and loving family that being in their midst made me feel the contrast to my relationship with my only living brother more starkly. I wondered how my mother had endured the loneliness of living in a foreign land all those years, in another culture, without her extended family.

In our honor, Soong-Mo and her two daughters cooked a familiar feast—all the foods my mother used to make. On the low table were set jap-chae, bulgogi, three kinds of kimchi, and seaweed soup—all comfort food, prepared in the Northern regional style. My mind flashed back to the last Christmas dinner my Omai had prepared for her small family. I remembered her tiny kitchen, hot with the stove's four burners in use. She made our favorite dish, mung bean pancake, from scratch, a process that is very labor-intensive. Every now and then, she sat down on her kitchen chair to catch her breath. That was a feast. Who knew she would die twenty-three days later?

Soong-Mo motioned to my husband and me to sit around a table already set with a variety of panchan (appetizers). The sons also joined us at the small table. The women, including my aunt, sat behind us, watching and serving us. I had forgotten how the system worked. Men were served first; then the women ate the leftovers. I was an exception—in memory of my mother.

At the dinner table, my husband had the easiest time, since no one expected him to speak Korean. He was elevated to a higher status as an honored guest—he met all the criteria: he was male, old, a professor, an American. I, on the other hand, struggled to converse articulately. I didn't possess the requisite vocabulary befitting a middle-aged person. In talking with my relatives, I realized that my mother and I had very largely invented our own version of Korean-English.

After dinner, all of us sat on the floor of the living room except for Lee. My male cousins insisted that he sit on the sofa. They practically lifted him off the floor and placed him gently on it. I was amazed at Soong-Mo's agility. She could squat for a long time and sit on the floor without any trouble. I, on the other hand, had to constantly shift my position, as my legs and feet kept going to sleep.

Even though the air was thick with the specter of my mother, no one broached the subject. I was hesitant to mention anything, as I did not want to offend my relatives.

But soon, Soong-Mo helped me out. She noticed the small suitcase I had placed near the shoes at the entryway. "What do you have in there?" she asked.

"I brought Omai's clothes," I replied. And then I felt at a loss for words. I fetched the suitcase and placed it in front of her. I snapped open the lock. I lifted the lid.

Soong-Mo rescued me from my clumsiness. She took one garment out and pressed it to her chest. My tears welled up, seeing this loving gesture.

"We need to burn your mother's clothes so that she has clothes to wear in the spirit world," she said quietly.

"Yes. Omai told me that was the custom. But I didn't know where I could burn her clothes, where I live," I said to her in my childish Korean. In truth, I didn't know the ritual at all. How was I supposed to do this burning of my mother's clothes? Was I to burn them in my Weber BBQ grill?

"I will take care of the burning," said Soong-Mo as she folded her sister-in-law's clothes and set them in a neat pile.

Soong-Mo reminded me of my mother. She could take care of anything. She'd make sure my Omai would be clothed in the afterlife. I felt comforted and yet relinquishing my mother's clothes felt like loosening my grip on her hand, when I was a little girl.

JEONG

May 12, 1996

THAT SUNDAY, HONG BOK's family attended the Mass and Hong Bok taught Sunday school. The stately Myeongdong Cathedral was the only building still standing from 1950, before the war. Upon entering, I automatically searched for the holy water fonts. When I located the nearest one, I dipped my fingers in the water and blessed myself with the sign of the cross. Holy Mass was over, but parishioners were still sitting in the pews or kneeling in prayer. I slid into the third pew from the altar. A scene surfaced in my mind, of my First Holy Communion: I saw the white veil and white dress I had worn.

In the quietness of the church, I was transported to that year: the year before the war. Every Sunday, my mother would dress me in my Sunday best, a blouse and a starched skirt pressed to perfection. We would walk to the church, but on cold winter days, she gave me piggyback rides, covering me with a heavy blanket so that no one could see me. I'd ask her from under the blanket, "Are we almost there?" and "Just a little bit longer," she'd reply. She knew to let me down a block away from the church, as I didn't want people to see me riding on my mother's back at my old age of eight.

A year later, the war was raging, and attending Mass on Sundays became more urgent. Everybody prayed, even Little

Brother, my second brother. My mother tricked me into attending Mass by carrying me on her back, but she couldn't get her second son to attend. He was simply never enthusiastic about getting up early for Mass—until one Sunday morning when, to our surprise, he was not only up in time but was the one hurrying us to go. We arrived at the church, but when Mass was about to start, he was nowhere to be seen. After Mass, we went outside to look for him. My brother came rushing up to us with a wide grin and waited for us to ask the expected question: "Where were you?"

He couldn't contain himself. He chuckled and put his arms around our mother, glancing around to make sure no one was eavesdropping. "See that jeep over there?" He pointed to an army jeep. "I took it for a drive," he whispered.

Mother moved out of his embrace and clasped her hand over her mouth. "You shouldn't do that! You are going to get in trouble!" She pointed her finger at him.

"An-nee-ya. (No way.) Don't worry." He patted our mother's shoulders. "I brought it back in time, didn't I?" He crossed his arms and smiled.

After that, he went to church with us every Sunday. While the American GIs were attending Mass, my brother revved up one of their jeeps and took it for a ride. This was one small pleasure available to a seventeen-year-old boy during that dismal time of war. I smiled at the memory of my brother driving a "borrowed" jeep. Now, visiting this landmark cathedral, I knelt and prayed for the souls of my mother and Little Brother.

THE TRAFFIC IN SEOUL, even on a Sunday, was gridlocked. Cars moved en masse as if they were locked together, sometimes three abreast, sometimes four. No driver paid attention to the lines—if there even were any. Hong Bok maneuvered in and out. He'd get close enough to another driver to touch him, crank his window down, stick his head out, and speak, at the same time gesturing which direction he wanted to go. Horns honked continuously. Being a passenger was nerve-racking, especially for my husband, who sat in the front seat as the honored guest.

Throughout this excursion, my mother was on my mind, keeping me company as if she were sitting on my shoulder. We passed the Olympic Stadium and the sight brought more memories of my mother to the surface.

Many years ago, when we first arrived in Los Angeles, she and I walked to the Memorial Coliseum from our rented house on Jefferson Blvd. Images rose in my mind of the route we walked, the landmarks we passed, the car dealership with the Felix the Cat figure on its roof. When we reached the Coliseum, I saw the Olympic symbol above the portal: five interconnected rings.

We walked around the huge stadium hand in hand, as my mother told me all about the Olympic Games, how it was an international sports competition held every four years in a different city, how all the countries in the world sent their athletes to the Games. Then she stopped talking and fell silent for a moment, sinking into her own thoughts. I waited and after a while she started speaking again. "The Games of 1936—that was a sad time for us Koreans."

"Why, Omai? Why was it a sad time for us?"

"Because the Weh-nom were still occupying Korea." Weh-nom was a derogatory term for the Japanese. When I heard it, I knew the snippet of history she was about to tell me was distasteful to her. "The athletes who competed in the games were representing their country. That year, a Korean man named Kee Chung Sohn won the marathon, the long-distance race. All the Koreans cried because he had to run the race wearing the rising sun emblem of Japan." My mother sighed. Her bosom rose and descended with a heaviness that matched her mood.

"Kee Chung Sohn hated the idea of wearing the Japanese flag. He did not want to compete for a country that enslaved his countrymen. He washed the enemy's emblem again and again until the red sun became a faded circle," she said. "As he stood to receive his gold medal, he heard the band play the Japanese national anthem. That's when he cried. We all cried."

Hearing this story from my mother, I, too, wanted to cry.

Fifty-two years later, the Olympics of 1988 were held in Seoul. I turned on the television just in time to catch an old man running with the Olympic torch held high. The announcer said the man's name: Kee Chung Sohn! The man who had won the Olympic gold medal in 1936. I called my mother on the phone. "Omai! The mah-rah-son man is on TV. Turn on your set."

We watched our respective televisions, sharing our comments on the phone, my mother and I, that September day. We watched the Olympic gold medalist run once again, this time as an old man, but this time carrying the Olympic torch and running for his own country, for Korea. We saw him running with all his strength and all his love for his country. He was transported that day to his young self. When he lit the cauldron accompanied by the Korean national anthem, my mother and I couldn't help but cry tears of joy for this athlete and for our native land. We held onto our phones for a long while, my mother and I.

I tucked these thoughts back into my mind and took a good look at the Seoul Olympic Stadium before me. As my cousin slowly drove around it, bittersweet remembrances mingled with unsettled emotions, creating a heavy weight in my thoughts. I found I was a different kind of tourist—one for whom these sites were entry points to emotions I was struggling to resolve.

We took a ferry, next, to cruise the Han River, which bisects Seoul. Since there weren't four seats together, my aunt and I had to sit apart from the others. I was glad because it would give me an opportunity to ask her some questions privately.

The boat had rows of long wooden benches on each side and an aisle in the middle. I led my aunt to a space nearest the wide window and sat next to her. Four other passengers were already seated there, and with these other passengers close enough to listen, I didn't know how to broach the subject of my birth. I waited for an opportune moment.

The passengers all settled in their seats, and the boat was starting to take off. The noise of the engine would make it impossible for others to hear our conversation. This was the opening I needed.

"Soong-Mo," I blurted. "I know how I was born." I didn't know how else to begin.

If she was startled by my revelation, she did not show it. She just looked at me without expression. "Who told you?"

"My brother."

"He shouldn't have told you." She shook her head and muttered something I didn't catch. The ferry chugged along the drab river. We sat looking out, the scenery just a backdrop to our separate thoughts.

"It's long forgotten, and it doesn't matter," she said, and fell silent. I waited. I studied my old aunt's face. She was deep in thought, far away. She looked down at her folded hands. How much she reminded me of my Omai!

"I would never have discussed this with you, but since you already know, I feel I can." She gazed at me, her once-big eyes now hooded with heavy lids. "Remember that your mother was only thirty-three years old when she lost her husband. That fact should explain everything."

She took several breaths and looked out the window. Then she addressed me again. "After giving birth, your mother told your brother and others that she was adopting a baby. In the beginning, your brother liked you. But one day, your mother's younger sister, Soong-Bong, told your brother the truth about your birth. From then on, I could see, his feelings toward you changed. That is the real reason why your mother and her son never got along."

I asked her if the folks in Unryul discussed this and was it a great embarrassment for my mother as well as the family. She shook her head. "Ahn-nee. (No.) Only the family knew."

"But my brother's wife said that everybody talked about this scandal." I pictured On-nee's grim face that horrible first evening in Japan; I'd cringed when she'd bellowed the words.

"That woman! She should not say such a thing." My aunt's nose flared, and her eyes showed a glint of anger.

"Your elder brother never acknowledged or appreciated the work, the effort, the devotion his mother showered on him. Here is just one example. When we lived in Unryul, your mother caught a stray chicken one day. Because it was a stray, she fed it to the others, but not her son. Her son got the best food."

My aunt was a woman of few words, but this topic had touched a nerve. Softly, almost as if she were talking to herself, she muttered, "It's a shame they did not have a chance to resolve their differences before your mother passed away." She looked out the window.

Hong Bok and Lee were looking back at us and smiling. The boat had rounded the bend and was on the other side now, returning. My aunt must have felt more at ease because she now shared a family story I had already heard from my mother in the late 1970s when the event occurred; I had just heard the story again, a different version of it, from Big Brother in Japan.

"Your brother owned several houses in Seoul many years ago," my aunt said. "Since he and his family lived abroad, those houses were vacant and in need of repair. That was a time when my family was very poor, the children were still young, and we did not have a permanent place to live. We lived in a makeshift shack with a corrugated metal roof—a temporary arrangement. Those shacks were up in the mountains and when rain came, it was impossible to live there. Mud was everywhere. In wintertime, they were uninhabitable.

"When your mother learned of our plight, she told us to go live in one of your brother's houses. We were so grateful to have a home that we made repairs and additions to the house. We even turned one section into a store, where I sold goods. Then, after we had fixed up the house, your brother began to worry that we would become squatters."

I could see my aunt's measured breaths by the rhythmic rising and falling of her chest. I already knew the aftermath of this story.

"So, one time when he was in Seoul, he told us to vacate. We didn't have any other place to go, but that was not his concern. He contacted a man named Ho to sell the houses."

My aunt bit down hard on her false teeth. "After the sale, we were evicted. Your uncle wrote to your mother and she tried to intercede with your brother on our behalf. But we never heard from your brother. As it turned out, he sold the houses for a pittance. If he had kept them and let us stay there, if they were still his, he would be a rich man now, since property values in that area have gone up so much since the sale." She clucked her tongue. "Tsk, tsk," she summed up, and shook her head.

Later, I thought about the three versions of this story. For my aunt, the story showed what kind of a man my brother was: heartless. She did not say it outright, but this was her view. Then, there was my brother's version. He felt that he'd been wronged, that his uncle had taken advantage of him. As for my mother, she was caught in the middle. I was reminded of something my mother had said about her own eldest brother years before: "He only cares for his own immediate family." I also recalled her saying, "Your eldest brother is just like my eldest brother." I couldn't remember when she uttered these words, but it might have been when her son evicted her brother and his family from the house he owned.

MONDAY WAS OUR FINAL day in Seoul. My cousin, Hong Bok, had been working hard to conduct his business while also acting as our tour guide. Often, he dropped us off at some site and let us tour on our own. When we returned at the designated time, we'd see him waiting for us with a cigarette between his fingers.

On this, our final day in Seoul, he was planning to devote his entire day to us. He was taking us to the DMZ, the 38th parallel demilitarized zone that divides the two Koreas. It is a dead zone 160 miles long and 2.5 miles wide, flanked on either side by the most heavily militarized border in the world.

Hong Bok started the tour by taking us to the Korean Foundation to meet a cousin three or four times removed.

We knew he had to be related to us because he and Hong Bok shared the same middle name, just like siblings.

My cousin rose from his chair and rushed to greet us when we entered his office. In that familiar Northern dialect, he said, "Dong-saeng (Little Sister), welcome!"

I bowed to my cousin, addressing him with the name that means "Cousin-Brother" in Korean. I asked him if he remembered me from so many years ago, when I was a toddler and he was an eleven-year-old boy. Back then his family had lived within walking distance of my maternal grandparents' home.

He gazed at me, his eyes searching for a remembrance of the past. "Yes, of course, I remember you!" he said. "You were the round-eyed girl always clutching your mother's skirt. You both visited us often. We called you Gong-dai, the Tail. Everyone knew your mother was the head and you were the tail. You two were inseparable."

We left the congested city traffic of downtown Seoul for the one-hour drive north to the DMZ. The closer we came to the demilitarized zone, the more surreal everything appeared. Vast stretches of open land that could have been verdant agricultural land were stripped bare as a result of the military standoff.

Even with my two cousins as guides, I felt nervous. I had read about the North Korean side's many attempts to provoke South Korea, ever since the DMZ had been created by the Armistice Agreement of 1953. Inside the building, the South Korean soldiers stood like statues, but I could feel their eyes watching every move from behind their dark glasses.

We stood at the lookout point looking north beyond the densely forested demarcation. My cousin-brother came here often, I learned, especially on holidays. This place, so stark and forbidding, was the closest he and others like him could get to North Korea, to places they'd fled so long ago. They came here and cried. They came here to mourn the homeland they would never return to. The other side is visible to the naked eye from that lookout point. It's right there and yet it's as distant as the moon for displaced North Koreans.

Inside the building, there was a large bulletin board filled with handwritten messages tacked onto it. At my side, my cousin-brother read some of the messages aloud. Poignant messages expressed longing to see loved ones. Visitors could write their own messages for the unification of the two Koreas on the printed forms stacked on the table. I picked up the small sheet of paper and in my best handwriting wrote in Korean: Han Gook ee hahn narah dweh ghi ro gheedo hahm ni dah: I pray that Korea will be one country again. I knew that this plea to God had been on Omai's top ten list of prayers.

Hungry to know about the life I had lived in our hometown, I clung to my cousin-brother's words, even though I had difficulty comprehending his Korean. He told me my family's land holdings were ten by twenty miles—about the size of Lake Tahoe, I calculated. Before the Communist takeover in 1945, landed gentry like my family had sharecroppers working the land.

"How far is Unryul from here?" I asked.

"About 200 kilometers north," he said.

Just 120 miles north of the DMZ lay the village where I was born. So close, the homeland to which none of us would ever return. Even our remembrance of it had been pulverized by political events and scattered like ashes.

As if he could read my thoughts, my cousin-brother took both my hands in his. "Dong-saeng," he said, "Little Sister: inasmuch as we cannot be with our family in North Korea, we appreciate the family we have with us here. I am very happy that I am reunited with my Dong-saeng. You are precious to me."

It was then that my tears began to flow. I cried because I could not express the fullness of my emotions with words. Only with tears, that primal solace of humanity, could I begin to reciprocate my cousin-brother's sentiment.

We stepped outside and walked along a designated path. On the wire fencing bordering the path hung long colorful strips of cloth. Each colored ribbon bore written messages from those who had families in the North. At first sight those ribbons looked festive, but when you came closer, they looked wilted and tired. So many families had been torn apart when this country was divided. Mine was one of them.

Farther on, there stood a dilapidated wooden bridge. Its rusty panel marker denoted the Military Demarcation Line between the two Koreas. Seeing it, I felt a chill running through me, even though the day was warm. After the war, the captured North Korean soldiers were given a choice—they could walk over to the North or they could stay in the South. If they chose to walk across that bridge to the North, they could never return, thus the name: Doraol su eomneun dari. The Bridge of No Return.

For me, bridges are connectors, like my favorite, the Golden Gate Bridge, which spans the bay from San Francisco to Marin. Bridges should be like helping hands, making it possible for a person to cross to the other side. Here, however, was a different kind of bridge. Instead of fostering hope, it caused despair; instead of bringing loved ones together, it tore them apart. My heart felt suri-suri: scoured with the aching sorrows of all the families this bridge had ripped asunder.

We made one more stop: the Korean War Memorial Hall. At the entrance stood a life-sized statue of two soldiers

embracing each other. My cousin explained that the two soldiers were brothers, one fighting for North Korea and the
other for South Korea. They chanced to meet on the battle-
field. For me, at that moment, the bronze statues turned into
flesh, blood, and tears. If they had not been on a pedestal, I
would have thrown my arms around those brothers. My body
ached with all the unspoken words and tragedies of war. I
remembered a moment I witnessed forty-six years ago when
a sister and her brother stood facing each other, looking like
statues because they had to pretend to be strangers, in what
must have been one of the most heartbreaking moments of
my Omai's life. Her words now rang in my thoughts: "I didn't
even get to touch his hand."

In Japan, time had seemed to crawl. In Korea, it sped by
fast. On our last evening, for a farewell dinner, Hong Bok
took us to an American restaurant housed in a hotel that
catered to foreigners. It was sensitive of him to choose this
restaurant, I thought: he chose it as a favor to Lee, for we had
been eating Korean cuisine at every meal.

At dinner, with the statue of the two brothers still fresh
in my mind, I said, "I don't know how families can cope with
the lifetime of separation that wars create."

Hong Bok took out a pen from his breast pocket and
wrote a Chinese character on a napkin.

"On-nee," he said, "do you know the word 'jeong'?" It
was polite of him to assume I even knew the sound of this
word, much less the Chinese character for it.

"Does it mean love?" I guessed.

He pointed to the two parts of the Chinese character.
"These strokes mean 'heart' and these strokes mean 'blue.'"

I wanted to understand but I couldn't put the two con-
cepts together. Heart and blue. "Heart must have the same

meaning in Korean as in English," I said, "but blue? Blue is a color. Does it have another meaning too?"

"Blue is the color of the sky on a bright day. When we have jeong, the heart is bright like the blue sky," he said, smiling. "Jeong encompasses love, but in Korean, it has a broader meaning: love, endearment, loving sentiment, affection. And attachment."

Yes, I understood jeong. I could not define it with just one word in English but I could feel it. When you have jeong, you feel an eternal connection, an invisible bond that extends beyond space, endures beyond time.

"We have jeong," my cousin said, putting his arms around my husband and me.

I repeated his words: "My heart is bright when we have jeong."

Maybe that was the problem between my mother and her firstborn son. No jeong.

PART 5

BACK HOME

MOTHER AND ME
REVISITED

California, 1996

COMING BACK FROM KOREA reminded me of something my mother often said whenever something chaotic ended: "Kūt geut nango kah teh. (It seems kūt has ended.)" As a child witnessing the kūt ceremony held for my sick grandfather, I had run in terror as fast as I could away from the ominous thundering of drums that accompanied the shaman's frenzy.

At home, sitting comfortably in my dining room alcove, I found myself repeating Omai's words: Kūt geut nango kah teh. No more metaphorical banging of drums, clanging of cymbals, or wailing by the mudang. But what lingered was far more tumultuous.

My two-week journey had changed my relationship with my mother. That first evening at my brother's home, I had uttered in shock: "How could she?" and Big Brother's answer pounded in my head throughout the days that followed: "She had her needs." Like a theme in a fugue, Omai's secret coursed through my days, although the only sign of my inner turmoil was tears I occasionally let slip down my cheeks.

I never imagined I'd feel nostalgia for those months of mourning before I knew my mother's secret, the all-encompassing sorrow of those days. Only after I returned from the trip did I grasp the emotional nourishment that pure, uncomplicated grief can give.

FOR MANY WEEKS, EVERY time I looked in the mirror, I saw my Omai's face. I couldn't tell what specific features I had inherited from her, but there she was, looking right at me from the mirror: my mother. Peering at that familiar face, I uttered again and again what Omai would have said: "Har su up suh yo." It cannot be helped. It was her signature saying whenever we reached a dead end.

On one of those days when I felt most conflicted, I opened the Bible. The first page I came to was Matthew 7. I read the lines: "Judge not, that ye be not judged. . . . Why beholdest thou the mote that is in thy brother's eye, but considerest not the beam that is in thy own eye?" Mote. Beam. I felt the beam in my own eye.

What would I have done in her predicament, given the context? Korean culture was steeped in the teachings of Confucius. As a widow, my mother knew what the script would be for the rest of her life. She belonged to her deceased husband's family. No matter how lonely she felt, they needed her to remain a widow. It would be her duty to serve and keep serving her parents-in-law until her firstborn son married, at which point she would earn the right to become the mother-in-law, the culminating role of her life.

What would I have done in her place?

When my mother bore a child out of wedlock, she plummeted from the respected position of widow to the gutter lot of shameful women. How much easier it would have been for her to flush me down the river. And she could have done it: no one would have been the wiser. In Korean culture the one thing worse than death is to bring shame upon one's family. A person who does that must live with the consequences for all her remaining days. My Omai took that fate worse than death upon herself, and because she made that choice, I am alive today.

This came home to me one day in June, when I made my way to a place I had visited countless times with my mother: Loma Linda University Medical Center. For over a decade, she and I had standing appointments with her doctor there. Our routine was always the same: I would park the car in the loading zone in front of the building, get out, retrieve her walker from the trunk, and open the passenger-side door. Omai would steady herself by gripping the inside handle above the car window with her left hand. When I reached out to help, she would refuse my offer. She'd say she didn't need help. Using her walker, she'd get herself to the bench in front of the building. I'd rush back to the car and find the closest open parking spot: I didn't want to leave her sitting there alone. When she saw me coming, she'd put her hands firmly on her walker, ready for our long walk to the elevators inside the building. A day came when she could no longer walk. How sad I was the first time she requested to be wheeled in: my independent mother, in a wheelchair. But soon, that became our routine, the new normal, and we honed it to perfection over the years.

That day, I was visiting the same doctor alone. How strange it was to sit in that waiting room without Omai. Usually, we would speak softly to each other in Korean, knowing that no one would understand what we said. Sometimes, she would make observations about other people in the room.

"Look at the woman over there," she'd say sotto voce. "She has a face like a slipper." No trace of a smile would

appear on her face as she said this. She could have been saying her Hail Marys. I, however, couldn't help laughing. Yes,
indeed, that woman's face was shaped like a slipper, with
two beady eyes decorating the top like buttons and a long,
rounded chin looking like the slipper's heel.

The nurse called my name. This felt strange. She called
my name, not Omai's, but it was her doctor I was seeing because I didn't have one of my own. After all those years as
Omai's translator, I regarded this doctor as our doctor.

When he knocked and entered the examination room, I
felt like I was on a first date. Without my mother present, the
doctor and I had to start from the beginning.

"How are you doing?" he asked.

"Doctor, I can't button my skirt. When I lie flat on my
back, my stomach isn't concave like it used to be. It's convex.
It feels hard." I poked my stomach with my fingers.

The doctor listened as I rambled on. I told him I looked
like a photo of a malnourished Biafra child I had seen in *LIFE
Magazine* years ago: scrawny except for a balloon-like stomach.
He examined me and then wrote something on a triplicate form.
"I am scheduling you for an ultrasound," he said.

How brave my mother had been. I was her translator, but
I didn't know the Korean words for most medical procedures.
"Omai," I would say, "you are going to have angioplasty," and
she would take it in calmly, even though she could not have
had any idea what an angioplasty was. Now, nothing was lost
in translation. The doctor and I spoke the same language: I
knew what he meant by an ultrasound. And I was scared.

On the day of the ultrasound, my daughter Julie went
with me. Suddenly, I was the mother, and my daughter took
on the role I'd had with Omai. My daughter—herself a doctor—accompanied me to the Radiology Department. I didn't

ask her about the procedure. I wanted her to think I was savvy about such matters—savvy in a way my mother had never been when I was the daughter.

A short man in a white coat approached to introduce himself. My mother would have given him a nickname, and he would not have known because she would have said it to me in Korean. I introduced my daughter to this man and immediately began bragging about her. "She's a doctor too!" My daughter tried to shrink, just as I had when my mother bragged about me, as she had done to anyone who spoke Korean.

As a professional courtesy, the sonographer invited my daughter to observe the examination. I lay on the examination table in my hospital gown. The ultrasound machine blinked images on the screen. The room was dark. I felt slippery stuff like Vaseline on my abdomen. I opened my eyes and looked at my daughter. Her attention was focused on the monitor. I closed my eyes again. The two doctors talked, using terms I didn't understand. This must have been how my mother used to feel. Why were they speaking to each other in such low voices? Whatever they were seeing, it must have been bad. I felt cold. I clenched my clammy hands as I waited to reclaim my body. After a while, the machine stopped humming.

"Come with me," the doctor said to my daughter. I opened my eyes and watched them walk out of the room, leaving me lying there, sticky and exposed. No one came to tell me what to do. I cleaned myself up and dressed and waited for my daughter in the waiting area.

Through a large window of the office, I saw her and the doctor studying the images on the computer screen. After what seemed a long time, my daughter joined me. Her eyes welled with tears as she sat next to me.

"There's a healthy blood flow to the ovaries," she said.

"That's good. Isn't it?" A healthy blood flow, she'd said. Healthy was a good thing, wasn't it?

"No," she replied. She hugged me, needing me to console her. At that moment, I became the mother again, and my daughter became a baby in my arms. I should not involve her in my medical issues, I thought. As a doctor, she knew too much: she couldn't treat her mother as a patient.

When I got my diagnosis, the only thing I was glad about was that Omai was not there to hear it. The news would have killed her: I had ovarian cancer. Suddenly, all my months of wallowing in self-pity, all my hurling of accusations at my mother's spirit in silent conversations seemed . . . childish. Over the next few days, researching my disease, I learned that ovarian cancer was the fifth leading cause of cancer deaths in women in the United States. Fifth place didn't sound too bad, but the article went on to state that ovarian cancer generally presented no symptoms until the cancer had spread extensively.

My months of pouting at the memory of my mother came abruptly to an end. I wanted my Omai. As a little girl, when I had stomachaches, she would put her warm hand on my tummy and massage away the stabbing pains. I wanted to be that little girl again: I wished for her hand upon me now. I was scared. And my fulminations wouldn't leave me alone. Why did I get ovarian cancer? Was it job stress that brought it on? Was it the estrogen medication? Was it some toxic chemical I was exposed to during the war? Oh, why didn't I have them remove my ovaries back when I had that hysterectomy?

The day my diagnosis came in, I saw my husband's face pale and I vowed I wouldn't die on him. When I married him, he was a widower whose first wife had died of ovarian cancer. She died at the very same hospital I would be referred to—the same hospital in which my Omai died. When he heard the words ovarian cancer, his gaze dropped, his shoulders slumped, and I felt the heavy weight of his thoughts. I lifted his face with my hands, I looked into his sky-blue eyes, and I whispered, "It will be OK."

From this point on, something changed. Instead of communing with my mother, I started channeling her. In hard moments, I asked myself, "What would Omai do?" I tried to be like her—strong, resilient. In mid-June, accompanied by my husband and daughter, I drove to UCLA to meet with my surgeon. I was shivering as I sat on a bench, waiting to meet him, but Dr. Montz thawed me immediately with his warmth, exuberance, and confidence. I had seen a lot of doctors and among them all, this one sizzled. Dr. Montz was a tall, slender man with his brown hair in a ponytail. He was wearing red clogs! The moment he smiled at me, I wanted to be his patient.

It turned out that Dr. Montz and my daughter had gone to the same medical school but in different years. I liked the professional camaraderie I sensed between them. After a physical examination, he spoke to the three of us. Surgery, he said, was the only option, but if I wanted him to do it, I would have to wait six weeks.

"Six weeks?"

Yes, it turned out. Six weeks hence was the earliest he could fit me in. During those six weeks, I felt the way prisoners on death row must feel as they're waiting for their execution days. I couldn't stop touching my bloated abdomen and imagining how big the tumor must be growing. At the end of each day, I marked another fat X on my kitchen calendar. I worried that I would catch a cold when the time came and be unable to get my operation. As July 12th approached, I spent my days obsessively cleaning my house.

I spent my nights negotiating with God, despite the strained relationship we had had at times. I confessed all my failings and promised to do better. In my previous promises to God, when I begged for a second chance, I promised to be a better student, a better educator, a better wife, a better mother. I promised to do better at the things I did. Now, I was telling God I wanted to be a good person. If I got a second chance, that's what I would strive for. My prayers closed with "Thy will be done."

The day before the surgery, my husband and I drove to the UCLA Medical Center in Westwood. It was a one-and-a-half-hour drive on Interstate 10. We didn't need to say anything to each other about the surgery—anything lovey-dovey would have seemed too much like a way of saying goodbye. Instead, while he drove, I told him what was on my post-surgery to-do list: learn to swim. Swim with the giant tortoises at Galapagos Islands. Learn to ride a bike. Run the Bay to Breakers footrace. Lee reached out to hold my hand.

In Westwood Village, I recognized familiar sights from my student days. Seeing the Landmark movie theater in the center of the village lifted my spirits. I had studied at UCLA, thanks to my Omai's insistence. There, I bought a robe from Macy's for my hospital stay. That night, Lee and I lay on our sides in the small, dark hotel room, my head cradled by his right arm and his left arm around my body nestled close to his. He whispered his nightly ritual: "Goodnight, sweetheart."

The next day, just before the anesthesia floated me into blankness, I appealed to my mother: "Omai, help me."

The surgery must have taken hours. But no one would have known it by the way Dr. Montz sauntered into the recovery room that evening with a mug of coffee in his hand. He sat next to my bed and smiled. He said he took out a cyst the size of a watermelon. He opened his hands to demonstrate the size. "You are a very lucky lady," he said. "The tumor was encapsulated inside the cyst so the cancer did not spread." Then he uttered the sweetest sentence I ever heard: "You will live to be a little old lady."

"How can I thank you?" I said. "You saved my life. Merely saying thank you doesn't feel like enough."

Dr. Montz reminded me that before my surgery I had told him I wanted to enter the Bay to Breakers run in San Francisco. He said I could thank him by sending him a picture of myself at the finish line every year. "That would be the best present you could give me," he said.

BAY TO BREAKERS RACE:
A CELEBRATION OF LIFE

San Francisco, May 1997

As LONG AS MY mother was alive, I measured time in infinite terms. "Someday" was always a given. In those days, running the Bay to Breakers had been an idea in my "someday" file.

The Bay to Breakers is one of the world's largest footraces and one of the oldest. The twelve-kilometer course starts at the bay side of San Francisco, near The Embarcadero, and ends at the breakers of Ocean Beach. Though I'd always vowed to run it, each year when the time came, the grind of daily life intruded, and I would sigh and tell myself, "Next year"—because back then there would always be a next year.

That July, I circled a date in my calendar. And on May 18, 1997—one year, four months, and one day after Omai's death—I ran in the Bay to Breakers race for the first time. I was fifty-six years old, and I didn't run the race to demonstrate my physical prowess but to harvest spiritual sustenance. I wanted to memorialize my mother and celebrate our life together—to celebrate life itself, in fact. Most of all, I did it as a way of thanking Omai for making me a survivor.

My son Eric picked up my husband and me early in the morning. It was chilly that day. Dense fog thickened the sky and the mist swirled at ground level. I couldn't see the city from the East Bay. Fog enveloped the Golden Gate Bridge as well.

I waited with tens of thousands of other runners in the starting area, predictably excited and anxious. My trainer—that is to say, my husband Lee—had devised a game plan. Since the route started at the bay, we would run the first three or four miles until we reached the Hayes Street hill, which some people call Hayes Street Hell because it is so steep. There, we would slow our pace to a walk, trudging uphill until we had topped the rise; after that, the rest of the way, we'd run.

At the starting line, the countdown began: five, four, three, two, one! A sea of sixty thousand people moved forward in a solid wave. Lee and I were caught up in the momentum. It was run or get trampled. Jockeying for space, we set our own pace. Runners were on the left side of the road, walkers on the right. I stayed behind Lee and focused on keeping up.

Along the race route, an assortment of musicians treated participants to blaring rock music. My favorite musical companions were drummers beating the bottoms of various-sized plastic containers turned upside down. The rhythmic beats commanded my feet to move.

Sights and sounds along the seven-and-a-half-mile route created a carnival atmosphere. There were many-legged centipedes composed of linked runners. There were Elvis impersonators and men dressed as nuns. There were jailbirds, nude men, nude women, and a variety of cartoon characters.

At every mile marker, encouraging words blasted out of megaphones. One cheerleader shouted, "You own the race!" I liked those words and chanted to myself, "I own the race, I own the race," as I huffed and puffed up a hill.

The course rounded a final bend and the last marker appeared. There, in Golden Gate Park, the gigantic surf of the Pacific Ocean came into view. It was just as breathtaking as the first time I had sighted that place where the endless ocean meets the San Francisco shore. That first time, I was approaching from the other direction: the breakers represented the end of a long sea journey. As my weary legs welcomed the finish line, my thoughts returned to the day my mother and I caught our first glimpse of San Francisco and its welcoming landmark, the Golden Gate Bridge.

October 1951. I was a ten-year-old immigrant from Korea, a country still at war. I had experienced bombs and hunger. I had endured the long ocean voyage, in a dingy four-passenger cabin, in the bowels of an enormous ship. The Pacific Ocean had seemed as boundless as the horizon, where dark blue waters met the vast azure sky.

My first sight of the bridge had taken my breath away. There it was, the gateway to my future, dressed in orange-red splendor, glittering in the rays of the sun—a stark contrast to what we'd left behind. Clutching my mother's hand that day, I stood on the deck of the ship as it glided toward the majestic structure, wondering if the boat's tall mast would clear the most beautiful bridge I had ever seen.

Forty-seven years later, those who had already finished the Bay to Breakers waited on either side of the finishing stretch, clapping, whistling, and shouting out encouraging words to the runners still coming in. Eric, who had crossed the finish line ahead of us, ducked under the rope to run with us. Taking my hand, he shouted, "You are almost there!"

With the thundering sound of the crashing waves, the wind from the ocean fanning my sweaty face, I grasped Lee's hand. With the two men in my life holding my hands, tears of joy and sadness overwhelmed me. As I finished the race, I shouted ecstatically, "Thank you, Omai!"

Running the Bay to Breakers that day, I celebrated the life my mother and I had sought all those years ago, when we came to America. My mother could no longer hold my hand, but my husband and son, with their firm grasps, had led me to the finish line.

I RAN THE BAY to Breakers every year after that. In August 2005, on my birthday, I set out to visit Omai, just as I had done every year since the year she died. My birthdays were always a big deal for my mother, even during the war. When we were living in a churchyard as refugees in Pusan, she planned a birthday party for me on the day I turned ten, inviting the neighbors living nearest to our tent. I was surprised when I saw fluffy white rice in our bowl: no one could afford to eat white rice then. Our typical meal was a watery gruel made of barley, with a few chopped vegetables added occasionally as a special treat. She had set out other dishes on the mat as well.

"I've invited our neighbors for your birthday," she said as she fanned the fire in the pit.

Her extravagance angered me. We didn't have any money and she was going to feed all these people? "I don't want a birthday party!" I shouted, as I turned away and headed to the far side of the churchyard.

I thought about that birthday many times in the years that followed. How I regretted my childish behavior after she died and I realized there would be no more birthday celebrations hosted by my mother. The last one was in August 1995, five months before her death; I was turning fifty-four. As always, in anticipation of my upcoming birthday, my Omai had painstakingly saved her money. I could visualize her, sitting on her wingback chair with a small woven bamboo basket on her lap, folding dollar bills. She had a unique way of doing this: she folded each bill in half longways and then folded it again and wove one end over the other, ending up with a tied knot. The basket was filled with dollar origami. She had been creating dollar origami for me for years, but I had taken it for granted—until there were no more.

I was marking my tenth birthday without her. I arrived at the Forest Lawn Cemetery late in the morning and drove slowly up the long winding hill to the Garden of Ascension, looking for my landmark, a prominent statue of a mother holding her child with the name Johnny Lail inscribed below it. My mother's plot lay to the left of that statue and up the hill a short distance.

Omai would have been proud of me that day. I bought flowers from Forest Lawn's shop, but instead of buying the green tin cone with a spike to use as a vase, I had brought along an empty mayonnaise jar and my cemetery tools: a small whisk brush, a hand shovel, a weed-picker, and rags.

I cleared the crabgrass surrounding her marker and swept away the remaining debris, and then polished the marker with a rag until the luster of the bronze metal shone. I traced the raised Korean letters with my index finger: Yung whun ee sahrang ha neun, Omoni, Halmoni (Forever Loved, Mother, Grandmother). I dug a hole near her marker and placed the jar of flowers.

Still kneeling, I told my mother that today was my birthday. On my children's birthdays, she had always said to them, "You should be celebrating your mother today. After all, she did all the work on your birth day!"

How I wished I had heeded her words and celebrated her on my birthdays. Is it always that way from one generation to the next? I asked her in my thoughts. Do we never gain insight until it's too late? How many times did I disappoint you? How many times did I hurt your feelings?

I imagined how lonely and scared my mother must have been, giving birth to an illegitimate baby. Were you alone? I asked her. When I delivered my firstborn, I was in a sterile, brightly lit green room with the obstetrician at my feet and nurses gently wiping my forehead. Even with all that help, I was panic-stricken about giving birth. Where were you, Omai, when I was born? How did you manage, knowing that no one in the world would be welcoming your baby?

I prostrated myself by her grave, placing my hands on her marker and addressing her with the honorific form for "Mother" in Korean: "Omonim," I said. "Does Omonim remember the first time I visited your grave? June 5, 1996, the day before your birthday. I was mad at you then, Omonim. I missed you so much, but I was mad at you. Visiting you that day was like the time you came for me at the orphanage. I was mad at you then, too. But now I realize I was mad because I was happy to have my Omai back. You see, all those days and nights at the orphanage, I longed for my Omai. I didn't have the luxury of being mad at you until I saw you.

"When I visited your grave that day, I was petulant like that little girl so long ago. I stood by your grave and told you that I forgave you, but I was forgiving you in order to white-wash your secret, which is now our secret. I wanted to bury it and keep it buried. Omonim, I was wrong. I am so sorry. Please forgive me for judging you, Omonim."

I thanked her for all the trouble she endured throughout her life, all the sugho: all the effort and labor and struggle and pain and trouble she went through.

"Omonim! Go mahp suem ni da," I said. Mother! Thank you! For my life, for the sacrifices, for keeping me, for raising me and protecting me.

"Until now," I told her, "I could not let you go because I could not bring our story to the finish line. I thought I was protecting you by keeping your secret buried. I could not let you go until I realized I was shortchanging you. Now, I can shout to the world how courageous you were, how much you loved me."

And so I let my mother go that day. I could because I knew at last the answer to the question I had never asked: Who is my mother? She is me. The essence of her lives on in me and through me. Who am I?

I am my Omai's daughter.

ACKNOWLEDGMENTS

I STARTED WRITING THIS book in 1996. My mother died, and writing my thoughts was a salve to my grief. I never imagined that my journal scribbles would turn into a book! Now 29 years later, with appreciation for the many persons who made writing this memoir possible, I worry that I will forget to recognize others.

Foremost, my heartfelt gratitude to Peg Alford Pursell, Publisher and Editor-in-Chief of WTAW/Betty Imprint, for accepting my manuscript, for having faith in my work, for nurturing me to believe in myself. As my editor, her perceptive contributions and sensitive reading preserved my voice. I am also grateful to my colleagues at Betty Imprint for their support: Leah Browning, Haley Hach, Janis Hubschman, Marianne Villanueva, Sharon White, Magda Bartkowska, Leah De Forest, Ilze Duarte, Kathleen Wheaton.

I am especially appreciative of California's public education institutions. Not knowing much about creative writing, I enrolled in writing courses at the Coronado Adult Education, Riverside City College, and University of California, La Jolla.

I was privileged to be in many writing groups. My thanks to all for their critiques, support, and camaraderie. I especially would like to acknowledge the contributions of the following writers: Michele Yepiz, Jenny Russell, Dr. Joanna Kraus, Reni Roxas, and Dr. Evie Groch.

Special thanks to my three beta readers: Dr. Flora Ida Ortiz for her insightful feedback on cultural and societal themes in the manuscript; Eric Brevig (my first-grade student in 1963 and current film director) for his constructive critiques; Dr. Leslie Kaplan, who went beyond being a reader. She copy edited and proofread my work in progress, and above all else, she is my "go-to" person for everything and anything pertaining to writing and publishing. I am indebted to her. Dr. Kaplan has published over a dozen academic books.

I am deeply grateful to author Gail Tsukiyama for inviting me to attend Napa Valley Writing Workshop. I am also grateful to co-teacher, author Jane Hamilton. The five-day workshop was a turning point for me. I felt like Cinderella at the ball.

My greatest thanks to author Tamim Ansary, my mentor, teacher, editor, and friend who took a rough draft and coached me ever so patiently and expertly to write this memoir. Without him, there would be no book.

Love and sincere appreciation to my family: my niece, Fran; my son, Eric; my daughter-in-law, Geraldine; my daughter, Julie; my son-in-law, John, and to my grandchildren, Jared, Evan, and Camille Helen who make me happy with their youthful exuberance. You inspired me to write this personal history. A special thanks to Eric, for his unwavering support, encouragement, and invaluable help with everything I ask, especially tech stuff.

Lastly, my heartfelt gratitude goes to my late husband, Lee. He cried each time he read a new section I composed of the manuscript. The Oshkosh, Wisconsin-born man thought he was that little Korean girl, Joanna Choi.

ABOUT THE AUTHOR

Joanna Choi Kalbus was born in North Korea. She made two critical migrations—from North Korea to South Korea after the Communist takeover, and then to the United States as a ten-year-old during the Korean War. She pursued her education in the United States, obtaining a PhD in Educational Administration, and has been involved in education for thirty-five years. *The Boat Not Taken* is her first book.

ABOUT BETTY

Founded in 2023, Betty is an imprint of WTAW Press, with a mission to publish books of prose by women for everyone. Betty aims to showcase and celebrate the diversity of women's voices.

By focusing on women's voices, Betty Books can contribute to a more nuanced understanding of women's experiences and foster empathy, understanding, and dialogue on important issues.

WTAW Press is a 501(c)(3) nonprofit publisher devoted to discovering and publishing enduring literary works of prose. WTAW publishes and champions a carefully curated list of titles across a range of genres (literary fiction, creative nonfiction, and prose that falls somewhere in between), subject matter, and perspectives. WTAW welcomes submissions from writers of all backgrounds and aims to support authors throughout their careers.

As a nonprofit literary press, WTAW depends on the support of donors. We are grateful for the assistance we receive from organizations, foundations, and individuals. To find out more about our mission and publishing program, or to make a donation, please visit wtawpress.org.